LEARNING TABLA

WITH

ALLA RAKHA

A MANUAL OF DRUMMING AND RECITATION

compiled by

Jeffrey M. Feldman

with Harihar Rao

Note: for a videotape of Alla Rakha playing the compositions in this book, contact DIGITALA

DIGITALA

N. Hollywood, California

DIGITALA
Box 4042
N. Hollywood, CA 91617

Printed in the United States of America

C O N T E N T S

Preface

This book is an introduction to the tabla as taught by Alla Rakha.
It is also Ustad Alla Rakha's introduction to his Punjab Style of solo tabla
performance, with its characteristic compositions and manner of striking
the drum. Alla Rakha selected the compositions to be included in the book;
the finger placement photographs are of Alla Rakha's hands, and the accompanying
tape cassette is a recording of Alla Rakha playing, reciting, and teaching
these compositions.

For many readers this book will also be an introduction to "tal," the
Indian grammar of rhythmic improvisation. If you are someone who appreciates
the rhythmic ingenuity of tabla players and would like to learn some of their
musical strategies -- even without learning to play the tabla -- then this book
was written with you in mind, as well as for the tabla student. The reader
who is content to learn the rhythmic solfeggio and theory can safely skip the
"Interchapters," which contain details of drumming technique.

Indian music and western musicians

A number of western musicians have incorporated Indian rhythms into their
playing, even to the extent of collaborating with Indian musicians. A few
examples are Yehudi Menuhin, John McLaughlin, the late Don Ellis, Tom Scott,
and Paul Horn. Western percussionists are well aware that drums have musical
potential beyond keeping the beat and imitating battle sounds. A few percussionists who have studied and applied Indian rhythm are Emil Richards, Ed
Shaughnessy, Collin Walcott, and John Bergamo. A study of tabla compositions
develops the sense of "linear" rhythm -- the feeling for long and complex
phrases. This Indian approach to rhythm can complement African or Afro-Latin
approaches, which emphasize the "vertical," contrapuntal sense of rhythm -- the

coordination of two or more contrastive movements.

The key to Indian rhythm is the "bol." A bol is a one-syllable name
for a drumstroke. When the bols are properly recited they take on the same
rhythm as the drum composition they represent. When the bols of a composition are memorized, they can serve as a basis of improvisation; bol phrases
can be rearranged, much as the phrases of a sentence can be rearranged. This
is the essence of Indian rhythmic improvisation; the speech capacity is enlisted
in the service of music.

The cardinal rule of Indian rhythmic improvisation is that the musical
phrases must fit into a recurring time frame called a "tal," a rhythmic
cycle. A tal is a cycle of accented and unaccented beats, similar to the
poetic meter underlying a line of verse (such as iambic pentameter). The
challenge to the musician comes in improvising without repeating himself or
losing track of the tal. To the novice this may seem a hindrance to free
improvisation, but to the master musician the tal provides a frame which
can be filled in clever and surprising ways. A notable example is the "tihai,"
a rhythmic device in which a single phrase is played three times, with the
very last stroke falling on the first beat of a new cycle. The phrases of
the tihai seem to go out of phase with the tal, only to mesh on the final
stroke with an air of finality. This sense of resolution makes the tihai
indispensable as a coda in Indian music, yet tihais are practically unknown
outside of India. Theoretically tihais could be used in any kind of music
which uses phrases of fixed length (such as the four-bar phrases of jazz,
rock, or marching drum cadences).

Another happy consequence of establishing a rhythmic cycle is that it
permits the musician to play at different speeds without affecting the overall
pace of the music. A good of example is the "tipalli gat," one of the compositions in this book. In the tipalli a phrase is played three times at succes-

sively faster speeds. The composition begins on the first beat of a cycle
and ends on the first beat of the next cycle, and may create an image like
a spinning coin that wobbles to a stop.

Reciting bols and keeping tal

The goal of the tabla player -- and of Indian musicians in general --
is to learn to move freely within the tal. The time-honored method for
achieving this goal is to practice at reciting bols while keeping tal. To
keep tal, the musician performs a recurring sequence of claps, waves of the
hand, and taps of the fingers, corresponding to the accented and unaccented
beats of the rhythmic cycle. The important point for the non-tabla player
is that learning Indian rhythm does not require learning to play an Indian
instrument. In India all singers, instrumentalists, and dancers learn to
recite bols and keep tal (although many supplement their rhythmic training
by learning some tabla). An added advantage of learning this rhythmic
solfeggio is that one can practice at any time, even when an instrument is
not handy.

Learning tabla from a book

Naturally the method of instruction offered here differs from the tradi-
tional apprenticeship in India. This book is a product of Alla Rakha's
classes in Los Angeles, offered during the summers of 1977 and 1978. To
accommodate his classes Alla Rakha condensed a year or more of intense
personal instruction into a dozen weekly classes, requiring the use of notation.
In India tabla instruction traditionally proceeds by the student's modeling
of the teacher, without aid (or distraction) of written materials. To satisfy
the teacher, the student must concentrate diligently to play each passage
exactly as it is demonstrated by the master. Through years of practice and
instruction, the teacher plays and recites longer and longer passages for

the student to imitate, stretching the student's span of attention and molding his sense of rhythmic form. Dependence on written bols is believed retard development. A student who yields to the temptation to jot down a few notes is liable to be asked by a wry master, "Doctor, are you writing me a prescription?" Nevertheless under the unusual constraints of limited time and of group instruction, it was decided that Harihar Rao would transcribe the compositions as they were dictated by Alla Rakha, and then the students would copy the week's lesson. Playing from transcriptions was discouraged, and each week the students were expected to have memorized the previous lesson.

The analytical approach

Nothing can replace Alla Rakha's presence as a teacher: first clapping the beat, then nodding approval, then correcting a finger placement, occasionally scowling like a man who has just heard an unpleasant noise, and often joining in on his tabla and beaming with delight. The reduction of Alla Rakha's lessons to print seemed to require a more analytical appoach than was normally used in class: the traveler without a guide needs a good map. Thus each composition is shown in three notational systems, including a diagram of its hierarchical phrase structure. Please take the diagrams in the proper spirit -- as learning aids -- and not as the only possible parsing of the music. The transcriptions and the diagrams are "pointing fingers;" as the Zen aphorism goes, once the finger has pointed at the moon, the finger is no longer of interest.

Acknowledgments

We have prevailed upon a number of good friends to contribute their special talents. Rone Prinz designed the cover and gave graphics help throughout the book (with an assist from Spencer MacDonald). Peter Manuel provided the Urdu calligraphy for the cover and made many useful editorial suggestions. George Landress composed the melodic interpretation of the First Kaida, which can be found in the Appendix. Zakir Hussain examined portions of the Interchapters and offered his own lucid description of the right hand technique, which was paraphrased and incorporated into the text. Mir Jacob played the melodic accompaniment on the recorded cassette. Harihar Rao, my first teacher of Indian music, assisted Khan Sahab in the classes and during the recording of the tape cassette. Richard Bock of the Ravi Shankar Music Circle engineered and edited the tape cassette, and gave more than one timely nudge toward completion of this project. Photographs by Jan Steward and Alan Ainsworth saved us thousands of words. And thanks, Mom, for the use of the typewriter.

This book would never have come about were it not for Pt. Ravi Shankar, who brought us Alla Rakha.

Alla Rakha and Ravi Shankar. (Photograph courtesy of Jan Steward)

Khan-Sahab with students from his Los Angeles classes of 1978.

Introduction

If your goal is to learn to play the tabla, simply begin with Chapter One and work your way through the book. If you wish only to learn Indian rhythmic theory and recitation, skip the Interchapters.

The tape cassette is organized like the book. Each new composition is introduced with a simulated lesson in which you will hear the proper recitation and execution. Next comes the entrance of the lehrā -- the melodic accompaniment -- and Alla Rakha recites and plays the composition at performance tempo.

The order in which Khān-Sāhāb presents these compositions is not the order in which they are played in a tabla solo. In the final chapter we "put Humpty Dumpty together again," and show the structure of the entire solo as it would be played in performance.

At the end of the book you will find a Pronunciation Guide, a Glossary, and an Appendix with suggestions for adapting these compositions for western melody and percussion instruments.

Listen to plenty of good music, and practice an hour a day. Have it!

C H A P T E R   O N E

Keeping Tal

A tal is a repeating pattern of accents. The corresponding English term is "rhythmic cycle." A tal can be visualized as the face of a clock.

Imagine a clock face that has been folded in half. At the top of the clock is sam (pronounced "sum"), the main accent of the cycle. At the bottom of the clock is khali, the secondary accent of the rhythmic cycle. One sweep of the hand around the clock, from sam to sam, makes one cycle of the tal. The sam marks both the end of an old cycle and the beginning of a new cycle.

The symbol for sam is the plus (+): the symbol for khali is the circle (o).

Folding the clock in half a second time gives two minor accents,

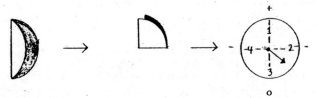

each of which is called tali. Tali means "handclap."

The symbol for tali is the dash (-).

Lesson 1.1   Keeping tal

Clapping to the rhythmic cycle is called "keeping tal."

Try this:

-Hold your left hand in front of you, palm up.

-On sam and tali, clap the right hand on the left palm.

-On khali, clap the <u>back</u> of the right hand on the left palm.

-Make each movement last 1 second.

-Count aloud from 1 to 4, one number per second.

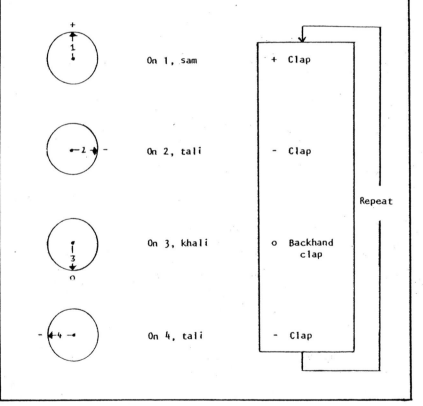

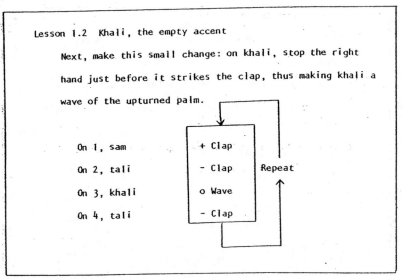

Lesson 1.2   Khali, the empty accent

Next, make this small change: on khali, stop the right
hand just before it strikes the clap, thus making khali a
wave of the upturned palm.

On 1, sam   + Clap
On 2, tali   - Clap   Repeat
On 3, khali   o Wave
On 4, tali   - Clap

Khali means "empty." Khali is the empty accent, the accent with no
clap. The rhythmic cycle "clap-clap-wave-clap" is called tīntāl, which
literally means "three-clap." Both methods of keeping tal -- with the
wave and with the backhand clap -- are in common use.

Lay is the Hindi word for tempo. If tal is the face of the clock,
then the lay is the speed of its hand. You have just been keeping tal
in "fast tempo," or drut lay, in which the sam comes every 4 seconds.
Next you will keep tal in medium tempo, or madya lay, in which a new cycle
begins every 8 seconds. Folding the clock face a third time creates
8 equal divisions.

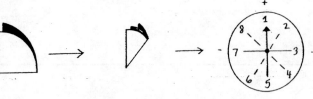

Lesson 1.3 Keeping tal: medium tempo

-Keep tal as you did in fast tempo, only make each movement twice.

-Make each movement last 1 second.

-Count aloud from 1 to 8 as you keep tal.

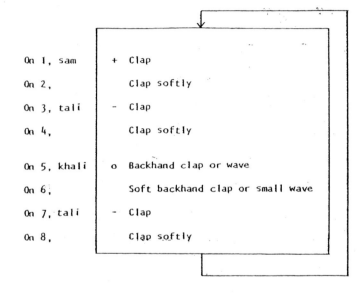

On 1, sam	+	Clap
On 2,		Clap softly
On 3, tali	-	Clap
On 4,		Clap softly
On 5, khali	o	Backhand clap or wave
On 6,		Soft backhand clap or small wave
On 7, tali	-	Clap
On 8,		Clap softly

Folding the clock in half a fourth time yields sixteen equal divisions of the cycle.

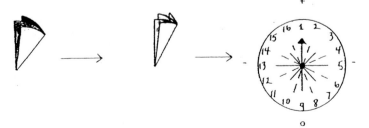

Lesson 1.4 Keeping tal: slow tempo

-Mark the accents -- sam, khali, and tali -- as before.

-On the first unaccented count after each accent, touch the right little finger to the palm of the left hand.

-On the second unaccented count after each accent, touch the right ring finger to the left palm.

-On the third unaccented count after each accent, touch the right middle finger to the left palm.

-Make each movement last 1 second.

-Count aloud from 1 to 16 as you keep tal:

On 1, sam	+	Clap
On 2		little finger
On 3		ring finger
On 4		middle finger
On 5, tali	-	Clap
On 6		little finger
On 7		ring finger
On 8		middle finger
On 9, khali	o	Backhand clap or Wave
On 10		little finger
On 11		ring finger
On 12		middle finger
On 13, tali	-	Clap
On 14		little finger
On 15		ring finger
On 16		middle finger

In slow tintal the 16 counts (or "beats") of a cycle are grouped into four "bars" or "measures" of 4 beats each. Each bar consists of an accent and all the unaccented beats which immediately follow it. The tintal cycle is often described as the rhythmic cycle of 16 beats divided 4+4+4+4.

Western musicians should be aware of the difference between a rhythmic cycle and a time signature. A time signature, such as 4/4, indicates the number of beats in a bar, but says nothing about the number of bars in a phrase of the music. One cycle of tintal is equivalent to a 4-bar phrase of 4/4 time.

"Odd" cycles. Incidentally, the bars of a rhythmic cycle need not be all of the same length, as they are in tintal: the 10 beats of the jhaptal cycle are divided 2+3+2+3. Nor must the tal be symmetrical: the 12 beats of ektal are divided 4+4+2+2, and the 7 beats of rupak are divided 3+4.

Tabla players say, "Once you know tintal, the other tals are easy." This may be like saying, "Once you make your first million, the second million comes easy"! In the lessons of this book, Alla Rakha follows the tradition of teaching only tintal to the beginning student. Once the principles of rhythmic improvisation and composition have been learned in tintal, they can be applied to any other tal and, in fact, to any form of eastern or western music which is organized in rhythmic cycles.

Hindi musical terms

Here are some musical terms commonly used by Indian musicians:

-A beat is called a matra.
-A bar or measure is called a vibhag.
-One cycle of the tal, from sam to sam, is called an avartan.
-Fast tempo is called drut lay.
-Medium tempo is called madhya lay.
-Slow tempo is called vilambit lay.

I N T E R C H A P T E R   A [1]

Tuning, Playing Position, and the
Strokes of the Tintal Theka

Tuning

Tabla teachers usually begin a lesson by tuning the student's tabla. The proper pitch for the dayan, the righthand drum, depends on its diameter. Dayans of 5 to 5½ inches are usually tuned to the C# in the second octave above Middle C. These are the customary drums for accompanying Indian stringed instruments such as the sitar. Larger dayans can be an inch or more greater in diameter and may be tuned as low as as the F above Middle C. These drums are often used to accompany vocalists. Dayans of any pitch can be used for tabla solos.

The dayan is brought into approximate tune by striking the tuning pegs with a small hammer. The tuning pegs are the wooden cylenders wedged between the body of the drum and the straps that hold the head in place. Hammering a peg raises the pitch; raising a peg eases the tension on the straps and lowers the pitch. The dayan is brought into fine tune by tapping the braided ring with the hammer. The braided ring is part of the head; tapping the top of the ring raises the pitch, and tapping the underside of the ring lowers the pitch. To test the tuning, the drummer strikes sur Ta, a stroke which is introduced in Interchapter B.

The pitch of the lefthand drum, the bayan, is not so critical. The head must be tight enough to resonate, but loose enough to permit the heel of the left hand to raise and lower the pitch with varying amounts of pressure.

---

1. If you wish you can learn to recite the rhythms without learning to play them on the tabla. If this is your intention you can skip over the "Interchapters."

PARTS OF THE TABLA

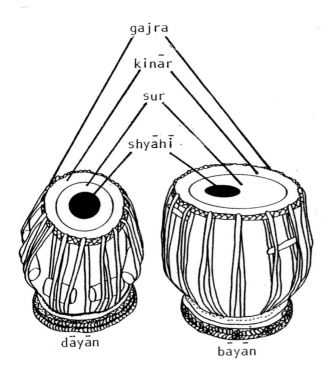

gajra

kinār

sur

shyāhī

dāyān   bayan

Playing Position

1) Sit cross-legged on the floor, or on a cushion (as Khan-Sahab sometimes does). Sit up, with a straight back.

2) (for righthanded players) Place the dayan on the ring in front of you and to the right. Place the bayan on the ring to the left. Leave an inch or two of space between the drums.

   (for lefthanded players) You can put the dayan on the left and the bayan on the right. As a matter of fact, dayan means "right" and bayan means "left," but never mind. From here on, read "right" as "left" and "left" as "right."

3) Tilt the dayan about 15 degrees away from your body and about 15 degrees toward the bayan. The bayan rests with its head parallel to the floor.

Starting position for the dayan

The hand positions described here are approximate, and must be modified to accommodate variations in hand sizes and tabla sizes; Alla Rakha's hands are rather smaller than average, and so players with large hands will have to adjust the most.

   1) Place the cushion of the right middle finger on the center of the shyahi (the black spot) of the dayan. The wrist is held as a natural extension of the forearm, neither bent nor turned.

   2) Place the thumb on the gajra (the braided ring). Place the little finger on the gajra or on the kinar (the circle of skin which forms the rim of the playing surface).

Starting position for the bayan

   1) Place the heel of the left hand on the center of the bayan. Rest the hand comfortably on the bayan head.

   2) Imagine a line which runs through the center of the bayan and also through the center of its shyahi. Rotate the bayan on its ring so that the middle finger falls on this line or a bit to its left.

The Strokes of the Tīntāl Thekā

Dayan Strokes

nā is probably the most frequently occurring stroke on the dayan. It has a clear, metallic sound struck with the index finger.

To describe hand positions, we will occasionally refer to the "axis." This is an imaginary line which runs from the elbow through the center of the drum head.

1) From the starting position, rotate the forearm, lifting the thumb, index finger, and middle finger from the drum. (The ring and little fingers remain in contact with the drum.)

2) Draw the forearm back along the axis until the cushion of the index finger is over the kinar.

3) Briskly raise and lower the wrist, snapping the cushion of the index finger on both the kinar and the sur (the exposed part of the head), and at the same time strike the thumb on the gajra.

The ring and little fingers remain in contact with the head through-out the stroke to dampen the low overtones. To produce the correct sound the index finger bounces on just enough of the kinar to give a sharp attack, and enough of the sur to give a pleasant reasonance. The thumb strikes the gajra for leverage. Alla Rakha makes a special point of this thumb technique, which is distinctive of the Panjab style. He will often show students his own right thumb, which has developed a large and impressive callous on the outer edge where it strikes the gajra.

In the exercise below, the strokes of each beat are underlined. The count is shown below the line. At a tempo of 1 beat per second, the notation indicates that 4 na's are played at 1-second intervals, followed by 8 na's at 1/2-second intervals. The double brackets (‖: and :‖) mean that the passage is to be played repeatedly, as an exercise.

Exercise A1   na

‖: na   na   na   na |na na   na na   na na   na na :‖
   1   2   3   4   5   6   7   8

  -Maintain a steady tempo of 1 beat per second.

  -Strive for clear, consistent tone.

Listen to the tape cassette for a simulated lesson in the strokes of the tintal theka, including na.

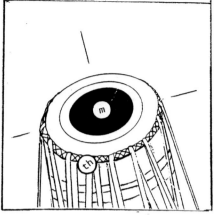

ti̅ is a dry tap of the middle finger cushion on the center of the shyahi.

1) From the na position, return the middle finger to the starting position. The ring finger does not slide on the playing surface, but rather rolls onto its tip.

2) Briskly raise and lower the thumb, index, and middle fingers, tapping the cushion of the middle finger on the center of the shyahi and striking the side of the thumb on the gajra.

Unlike na, in which the index finger bounces off the drum, the middle finger remains in place on the drum after striking ti, assuring a nonresonant sound.

na and ti alternate in the exercise below.

Exercise A2   na and ti   Tempo: 1 beat per second

‖ : na ti na ti | na ti na ti na ti na ti : ‖
   1   2   3   4   5   6   7   8

tin is a subtle, resonant stroke of the index finger on the sur and shyahi, to the left of the axis.

1) Assume the position immediately after striking ti. The ring and index fingers are in contact with the head, and the ring finger is bent. The cushion of the middle finger is over the center of the shyahi.

2) Rotate the forearm, raising the thumb, index and middle fingers off the head.

3) Briskly raise and lower the wrist, bouncing the length of the index finger on the sur and shyahi, and striking the side of the thumb on the gajra.

The ring and little fingers remain in contact with the head, dampening the low overtones. As with na, the high overtones are permitted to ring.

The following exercise incorporates all three of the right hand strokes used in the tintal theka -- the basic tintal rhythm.

Exercise A3   na ti tin na   Tempo: 1 beat per second

‖: na   ti   tin   na   │na ti tin na na ti tin na :‖
   1   2   3   4   5   6   7   8

-Strive for clear, consistent tone. The dayan rings continuously, except for ti.

Zakir Hussain, who is one of India's great tabla players and the son of Alla Rakha, offers one basic piece of advice on dayan technique: make every stroke the same way. The strokes na, ti, and tin are made with different fingers on different parts of the drum, yet all these strokes begin the same. First comes the rotation of the forearm, then the raising and lowering in turn of the wrist, hand, and finger, which snaps like the tail of a whip. Even as the finger strikes, the wrist rises in preparation for the next stroke, imparting a wave motion to the forearm, hand, and fingers. The hand and fingers maintain a slight bit of tension, making them stiff and springy. Furthermore the fingers are not merely thrown at the drum, but rather are placed firmly with every stroke, even at high speeds. (Note: Zakir illustrates this technique forcefully by squeezing the student's forearm. As a recipient of this demonstration, I can report that his fingertips dug deeply into my arm. Such a lesson can leave a lasting impression! -- J.F.)

(Photograph by Pierluigi Frassineti)

Bayan Strokes

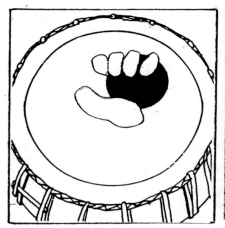 

ka (pronounced "kuh") is a dry rap of the knuckles of the left hand
on the shyahi of the bayan. It sounds something like a "sock" on
the pedal of a hi-hat cymbal. ka is played together with tin, which
gives tin a little more "sock."

1) Curl the fingers of the left hand into a loose fist.

2) Strike ka with the knuckles and fingernails, and at the same
    time...

3) strike tin with the right hand.

Exercise A4   na ti tin na with ka

Practice the previous exercise, na ti tin na , adding ka
each time you play tin.

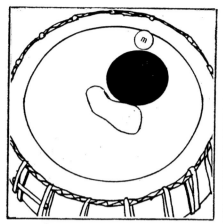

ge is a resonant stroke of the left middle finger (or occasionally the index finger). ge can be played with rising intonation (gé↗), falling intonation (gè↘), or neutral intonation (ge).

To strike ge (neutral intonation)

1) From the bayan starting position raise the left hand and fingers, leaving the heel of the hand in contact with the drum.

2) Bounce the tip of the middle finger on the sur, at the narrowest point between the shyahi and the kinar.

To strike ge↗ (rising intonation), add:

3) Press the center of the bayan with the heel of the left hand.

To strike ge↘ (falling intonation), change the order of the steps:

1) Press the center of the bayan with the heel of the left hand.

2) Raise the left hand and fingers, leaving the heel of the hand in contact with the drum.

3) Bounce the tip of the middle finger on the sur, at the narrowest point between the shyahi and the kinar, and immediately...

4) Release the pressure on the center of the bayan by relaxing the arm.

In the exercise below, ge↗ and ge↘ alternate.

Exercise A5   ge↘ ge↗

Tempo: 1 beat per second

‖: ge↘   ge↗   ge↘   ge↗ | ge↘ ge↗ ge↘ ge↗ ge↘ ge↗ ge↘ ge↗ :‖
   1   2   3   4   5   6   7   8

When ge↘ and ge↗ alternate at moderate-to-fast speeds, ge↗ is played with the index finger. In our notation we show this as ge↗$_i$, with the subscript "i" for "index." Similarly the subscript "m" stands for the "middle" finger, as in ge↘$_m$.

Exercise A6   ge↘$_m$ ge↗$_i$

Tempo: 2 beats per second

(This notation is the same as for Exercise A5)

Combined Strokes

A "combined" stroke is one which is struck with the right hand and left hand simultaneously.

dhī is a combined stroke of ti on the dayan and ge on the bayan.

dhin is a combined stroke of tin on the dayan and ge on the ba

A combined stroke may have neutral intonation, rising intonation, or falling intonation, depending on how ge is played. In the following exercise, dhi↗$_m$ is played as ti↗ and ge↗$_m$ simultaneously. dhin↘$_m$ is tin plus ge↘$_m$.

Exercise A7   na dhi↗$_m$ dhin↘$_m$ na

Tempo: 1 beat per second

‖: na   dhi   dhin   na :‖

You now know the phrases which make up the tintal theka, which is discussed in Chapter Two.

Exercise A8   The Beginner's tintal theka (Same as Lesson 2.1).

na dhi$_m$ dhin$_m$ na, na dhi$_m$ dhin$_m$ na, na ti tin na, na dhi$_m$ dhin$_m$ na

Tempo: 1 beat per second

+				-				o				-			
: na	dhi	dhin	na	na	dhi	dhin	na	na	ti	tin	na	na	dhi	dhin	na :||
1	2	3	4	5	6	7	8	9	10	11	12	13	14	15	16

When combined strokes occur in rapid succession, the middle and index fingers of the left hand alternate, as in Exercise A.6.

Exercise A9   The Beginner's tintal theka

na dhi$_i$ dhin$_m$ na, na dhi$_i$ dhin$_m$ na, na ti tin na, na dhi$_i$ dhin$_m$ na

Tempo: 2 beats per second

(This notation is the same as for Exercise A.8)

Dha$^-$ is a combined stroke of na on the dayan and ge on the bayan.

The tintal theka is normally played with a bayan stroke on every beat (except at khali), as in the following exercise.

Exercise A10   The Standard tintal theka: slow tempo (Same as Lesson 2.2)

-Ta is another name for na. The name "Ta" is used when the stroke takes the place of Dha$^-$ in the khali section of the theka.

Dha$_m$ dni$_m$ dhin$_m$ Dha$_m$, Dha$_m$ dhi$_m$ dhin$_m$ Dha$_m$, Dha$_m$ ti tin Ta, Ta dhi$_m$ dhin$_m$ Dha$_m$

Tempo: 1 beat per second

+				-				o				-			
: Dha	dhi	dhin	Dha	Dha	dhi	dhin	Dha	Dha	ti	tin	Ta	Ta	dhi	dhin	Dha :||

When the standard tintal theka is played at medium and fast tempos, the left index and middle fingers alternate.

Exercise A11   The Standard tintal theka: medium tempo

Dha$_m$ dhi$_i$ dhin$_m$ Dha$_i$,Dha$_m$ dhi$_i$ dhin$_m$ Dha$_i$,Dha$_m$ ti tin Ta,Ta dhi$_i$ dhin$_m$ Dha$_i$

Tempo: 2 beats per second

(This notation is the same as for Exercise A10)

Alla Rakha dictating a bol to Harihar Rao during a class at the East-West Cultural Center, Los Angeles, 1977.

CHAPTER TWO

Bols and the Tintal Theka

In Hindi, bol means 'word." Each stroke on the tabla has been assigned a one-syllable name. When these names are recited while keeping tal, they form a sort of poem which is an aid in learning drum rhythms. The word 'bol" may refer to an entire composition, to a short phrase, or to the name of an individual stroke. Most often, in the jargon of tabla players, "bol" means "composition."

A theka is a bol that shows the pattern of accents of a rhythmic cycle. The tintal theka is the bol that introduces the tal of 16 beats divided 4+4+4+4. Every tal has a distinctive theka, and a knowledgeable listener knows from the first couple of strokes which tal is intended. When playing a solo, the tabliya plays theka to introduce the tal, and then periodically returns to theka to re-establish the tal in the listener's mind. When accompanying a melody instrument, the tabliya generally plays theka, which serves as a "ride," as a jazz drummer would say. The tintal theka is commonly the first lesson on the tabla.

The Beginner's Theka

na   is pronounced as in English--rhymes with "Ma." On tabla, na
     is a high-pitched, bell-like ring. On a western drum set, a
     corresponding sound would be a stroke on the cone of a cymbal.[1]

dhi   is pronounced like English "dee," but with the tongue touching
      the back of the teeth (dental) and with a puff of air before and
      during the vowel (aspirated). Aspiration gives the vowel a
      breathy-voiced quality, like a stage whisper. On tabla, dhi
      is a dry tap and a simultaneous resonant "boom." On drum set,
      a corresponding sound would be a tap on the snare drum and a
      simultaneous stroke of the bass drum.

dhin is pronounced like the English "din," only the "d" is dental
      and aspirated. On tabla, dhin has a medium or low-pitched
      bell-like sound, accompanied by a simultaneous resonant boom.
      On a drum set, a corresponding sound would be a stroke on
      the body of a cymbal and a simultaneous stroke of the bass drum.

ti   is pronounced like the English "tee," only dental and unaspirated.
      That is, there is no puff of air after the release of the t and
      no breathy quality to the vowel. On tabla, ti is a dry tap.
      On drum set, it is a tap on the snare drum.

tin   is pronounced like the English "tin," only dental and unaspirated.
      On the tabla, tin is a medium-pitched bell-like ring. On the
      drum set, a corresponding sound might be a stroke on the body of
      the cymbal.

     In the following lesson, each beat is indicated by a horizontal line;
the number of the beat appears below the line, and the bol that is to be
recited or played appears above the line. For example, dhin means that
                                                         ‾3‾
the bol dhin comes on the third beat. When reciting and keeping tal, dhin
is pronounced just as the right ring finger touches the left palm. The
double brackets (||: and :||) mean that the bols between them are to be
recited over and over, with no pause between repetitions.

---

1. The drum set equivalents are offered to give an idea of the sound on the
tabla that the bol stands for, and is not necessarily the preferred sound
for transcription. See the Appendix for suggestions on adaptation of tabla
bols to western percussion instruments.

```
Lesson 2.1    The Beginner's Theka

        -Recite the theka while keeping tal at a slow tempo: 1 beat
        per second (see Lesson 1.4).

||:  +  na    dhi   dhin   na   |  na    dhi   dhin   na
        1     2     3      4       5     6     7      8

     o  na    ti    tin    na   |  na    dhi   dhin   na  :||
        9     10    11     12      13    14    15     16
```

Notice how the theka shows the tintal structure of 16 beats divided
4+4+4+4. The bol na dhi dhin na spans 1 bar (vibhag) of 4 beats (matras)
in length. The same bar is played 4 times, with a slight variation in the
third bar, the bar beginning with khali (o). The tabla player signals the
khali bar by not playing resonant strokes on the bayan, the bass drum
played with the left hand.

The Standard Tintal Theka

        The theka which you have just seen is Alla Rakha's first lesson but
is not exactly the theka normally used in soloing or accompaniment. In
the standard theka there is a bayan stroke on every beat (except in the
khali bar). In other words, na becomes Dha.

    Dha   sounds like "dah" except that Dha is dental (tongue
           against the teeth) and aspirated ("breathy"). On
           the tabla Dha sounds like a high-pitched ring and
           a simultaneous resonant "boom." On a drum set, Dha
           could be played as simultaneous strokes on the cymbal
           cone and bass drum.
               We capitalize Dha because of its importance. It
           is often the first or last stroke of a phrase.

    Ta   is pronounced "tah," only dental and unaspirated. On
           the tabla, Ta is played exactly as na. When a phrase
           containing Dha is played without its resonant bayan
           strokes, the syllable Ta replaces Dha. Therefore, we
           also capitalize Ta.

24

```
Lesson 2.2   The Standard Tintal Theka:  Slow tempo

              -Recite while keeping tal, or play on the drum, at
              1 beat per second.


    ||: +   Dha   dhi   dhin   Dha  | Dha   dhi   dhin   Dha
            ———   ———   ————   ———  | ———   ———   ————   ———
             1     2      3     4   |  5     6      7     8


        o   Dha   ti    tin    Ta   | Ta    dhi   dhin   Dha    :||
            ———   ———   ————   ———  | ———   ———   ————   ———
             9    10     11    12   | 13    14     15    16
```

Some fine points of playing and recitation. It is common to

play the very first stroke of the standard tintal theka as na, and

to play Dha on all repetitions. When reciting the theka, pronounce

beats 10 to 13 with slightly higher pitch than the rest of the theka.

These beats have no resonant bayan strokes. Beat 14, which marks

the return of the resonant bayan strokes should receive special stress

in addition to low pitch.

```
Lesson 2.3    The Standard Tintal Theka: Medium Tempo

               -Recite and keep tal, or play on the drum, at medium
               tempo, 2 beats per second.  If you are reciting, keep
               tal for medium tempo, 8 movements, 1 per second.  (See
               Lesson 1.3).

               -The notation for this lesson is the same as for
               Lesson 2.2
```

```
Lesson 2.4    The Standard Tintal Theka: Fast Tempo

               -Recite and keep tal, or play on the drum, at fast
               tempo, 4 beats per second.  If you are reciting,
               keep tal for fast tempo, 4 movements, 1 per second.
               (See Lesson 1.3)

               -The notation for this lesson is the same as for
               Lesson 2.2
```

INTERCHAPTER   B

New Strokes for the First Kaida

Khan-Sahab now introduces the bol tirikita, a 4-stroke sequence

of non-resonant taps which can be played rapidly.

1) From the starting position, raise the right hand and
   fingers from the dayan.

2) Strike ti with the middle and ring finger cushions. The
   middle finger strikes the center of the shyahi or a bit
   to the right of center.

Do not confuse this ti with the ti in the tintal theka, which is

played by the middle finger alone.

<u>ri</u> is a tap of the index finger on the exact center of the shyahi.

1) <u>ri</u> occurs only after <u>ti</u>. After striking <u>ti</u>, leave the fingers in contact with the d<u>ru</u>m.

2) Slide the index and middle fingers to the right, making a brushing sound.

3) Strike <u>ri</u> with the cushion of the index finger in the exact center of the <u>shyahi</u>.

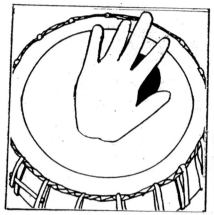 

ki is a pat of the open left hand on the bayan. This stroke
has a similar sound to the ka (Exercise A4) played with the knuckles
with tin. Generally, the stroke of the open hand occurs when ka, ki,
or ke is to be played alone; when played with tin, the stroke with
the closed fist is preferred.

1) From the bayan starting position, raise the flat hand from the
the wrist, leaving the heel of the hand in contact with the
bayan.

2) Strike ki with the open hand, giving a dry pat.

 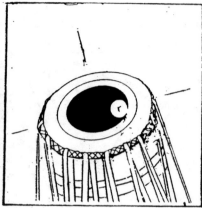

<u>ta</u> (or <u>t</u>) is a tap of the ring finger on the righthand side of the
shyani.

1) After striking ri, leave the index finger in place on the
   center of the shyahi while striking ki with the left hand.

2) Lower the right ring finger, striking ta ·

Exercise B1   ti_{mr} ri ki ta Dha_m

-Practice this exercise and the following ones at a slow tempo of
1 beat per second, then at a medium tempo of 2 beats per second,
and finally at a fast tempo of 4 beats per second.

-Make a clear, brushing sound between <u>ti</u> and <u>ri</u>.

$$\|: \underline{ti\ ri}\ \ \underline{ki\ ta}\ \ \underline{Dha}\ :\|$$

Exercise B2   Dha_ige_mti_{mr}ri ki ta Dha_m

$$\|: \underline{Dha\ ge}\ \underline{ti\ ri}\ \ \underline{ki\ ta}\ \ \underline{Dha}\ :\|$$

At this point you can turn to Chapter Three and learn the theme of the First Kaida and Variations I and II.

The following passage occurs in Variation III

Exercise B3: Dha ge ti ri ki ta Dha, Dhagetirikita Dha, Dhagetirikita

‖: Dha ge ti ri ki ta Dha,Dha ge ti ri ki ta Dha,Dha ge ti ri ki ta :‖
   1   2   3   4   5   6   7   8   9   10

  -In the exercise above, the commas have no time value; they only
  point out the boundaries between phrases.

This next passage occurs in Variation IV.

Exercise B4: Dha ge ti ri ki ta Dha,Dha,Dha,,Dhagetirikita Dha Dha Dha...

‖: Dha ge ti ri ki ta DhaDha |Dha,Dha ge ti ri ki ta Dha
   1   2   3   4   5   6   7   8

DhaDha,Dha ge ti ri ki ta :‖
 9   10   11 12

Here you can return to Chapter Three and learn the remaining variations and the short tihai. The following stroke, sur Ta, occurs in the chakradar tihai.

Sur Ta is played much like a loud tin (Exercise A3) only closer to the starting position.

However, this stroke functions in tabla solos more like Tā (that is, Dha minus the bayan stroke). The sur is the part of the playing surface which is not covered by either the kinar or the shyahi. The symbol for sur Ta is: Ťa.

When sur Ta is accompanied by a simultaneous resonant bayan stroke (ge), the resulting stroke is called sur Dha. The symbol for sur Dha is: Ďha.

In certain climactic passages, ti is played with two fingers on the sur:

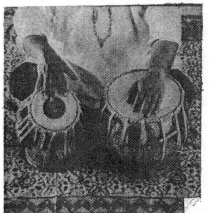 

   1) After striking sur Dha, raise the right hand off the dayan.

   2) Strike ti on the sur to the right of the axis with the cushions of the middle and ring fingers.

Another climactic strike is K't (sounds like "cut"), a dry swat of the open hand on the bayan.

   1) Raise the flat left hand from the bayan.

   2) Strike K't with the full open hand. The bayan is not permitted to ring.

The following passage occurs in the chakradar tihai:

Exercise B5: $\overset{*}{Dha}_m \, ti_{mr} \, \overset{*}{Dha}_m$ - - K't, ...

-The symbol - stands for a rest which is equal to 1 syllable in duration.

-Dha is played sur Dha ($\overset{*}{Dha}$).

-ti is played with two fingers on the sur.

$$\|: \underset{1}{\overset{*}{Dha} \; ti} \; \underset{2}{\overset{*}{Dha} \; -} \; \underset{3}{- \; K't,} \; \underset{4}{\overset{*}{Dha} \; ti} \; | \underset{5}{\overset{*}{Dha} \; -} \; \underset{6}{- \; K't,} \; \underset{7}{\overset{*}{Dha} \; ti} \; \underset{8}{\overset{*}{Dha} \; -} :\|$$

C H A P T E R   T H R E E

First Kaida: Dhage tirikita Dha...

Traditionally the first step in learning tabla improvisation is memorizing the theme and variation compositions of a master. The basic theme and variation is called kaidā, from the Persian word meaning "law" or "code." The law of kaida improvisation is that only bols of the theme may occur in the subsequent variations. Furthermore each variation must follow logically from its predecessors, so that the entire composition forms an integrated whole. A kaida development consists of three parts: a theme, a series of variations, and a tihāi.

The First Kaida features the bol tirikita, a sequence of dry taps which can be played or recited rapidly.

ti   is pronounced as in the theka.

ri   is pronounced as a flap of the tongue against the alveolar ridge (the ridge behind the upper teeth), like the middle sound in "butter" or "ladder" (in some American dialects) or like the British "r" in "very," followed by the "short-'i'" sound.

ki   is pronounced like the beginning of the word "kick," with an unaspirated "k."

ta   is pronounced retroflex (tongue curled back touching the roof of the mouth) and unaspirated, followed by the short neutral vowel ("uh"). Also written t.

ge   is pronounced like "gay," only without the ending y-glide. It is a resonant bayan (bass drum) stroke.

Lesson 3.0 First Kaida: Theme

-Recite and keep tal, or play on the drums, at the slow tempo of 1 beat per second.

| + | Dha ge ti ri ki ta Dha | Ta | Dha ge ti ri ki ta |
| o | Ta ke ti ri ki ta Dha | Dha | Dha ge ti ri ki ta |

Practice sequence:

Theka: 1 cycle at 1 beat per second [1]
Theme: 1 time at 2 strokes per beat
"   : 2 times at 4 strokes per beat

---

1. The lessons should be mastered at the practice tempo of 1 beat per second before playing at the performance tempo of 2 beats per second, as on the tape.

-The symbol - stand for a rest, a silent interval equal in duration to one syllable or stroke.

		na¹	dhi	dhin	Dha	‖ Dha	dhi	dhin	Dha	
o	Dha	ti	tin	Ta	Ta	dhi	dhin	Dha	(Theka)

+	Dha ge ti ri	ki ta Dha -	Ta -	Dha ge ti ri	ki ta	(Theme)
o	Ta ke ti ri	ki ta Dha -	Dha -	Dha ge ti ri	ki ta	

+	Dhagetiri	kita Dha -	Ta-Dhage	tirikita	(Theme:
	1	2	3	4	double speed)
-	Taketiri	kita Dha -	Dha-Dhage	tirikita	(Theme:
	5	6	7	8	double speed)
o	Dhagetiri	kita Dha -	Ta-Dhage	tirikita	
	Taketiri	kita Dha -	Dha-Dhage	tirikita : ‖	

Breaking a rhythm down into its phrases makes it easier to understand.

You can think of the theme as being made of two phrases of 8 strokes

each:

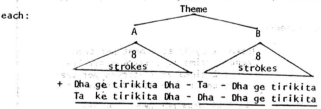

Like the theka, the theme has the structure of a poetic couplet: two rhyming lines of similar structure.

---

1. After the very first cycle of theka, replace this na with Dha.

At two strokes per beat, the 32 strokes of the theme span one cycle of tintal. Like the theka, the kaida theme signals the khali with the rhyme (and the omission of the resonant bayan strokes).

Variations

Lesson 3.1   First Kaida: Variation 1

-Spaces and commas have no time value: their function is to show structure

+   Dha ge   ti ri   ki ta,   Dha ge | ti ri   ki ta,   Dha ge   ti ri
     1   2   3   4   5   6   7   8

o   ki ta,   Dha ge   ti ri   ki ta | Ta -   Dha ge   ti ri   ki ta
     9   10   11   12   13   14   15   16

+   Ta ke   ti ri   ki ta,   Ta ke | ti ri   ki ta,   Dha ge   ti ri
     1   2   3   4   5   6   7   8

o   ki ta,   Dha ge   ti ri   ki ta | Dha -   Dha ge   ti ri   ki ta
     9   10   11   12   13   14   15   16

Practice sequence

         Theka: 1 cycle at 1 beat per second
         Theme: 1 time at 2 strokes per beat
         "   : 2 times at 4 strokes per beat
        Variation: 1 time at 4 strokes per beat

-For this variation at 4 strokes per beat, see the diagram below.

Variation 1, like all variations, is formed from phrases from the theme.

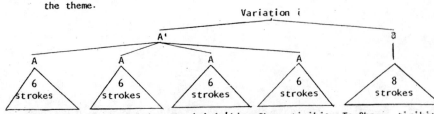

Variation 1

Each line of the variation consists of the first 6 strokes (or syllables) of the theme, played (or recited) 4 times, followed by the last 8 strokes of the theme, making 32 strokes in all. Kaida variations generally have twice as many strokes as a kaida theme, so the variations must be played at twice the speed of the theme. At that speed, the rhyme at the beginning of the second line of the variation corresponds with the khali of the rhythmic cycle.

The phrase structure of Variation I may also be expressed as

$$+ \quad (Dha \ ge \ tirikita)^4 \quad Ta - Dha \ ge \ tirikita$$
$$o \quad (Ta \ ke \ tirikita)^2_{2}$$
$$\quad (Dha \ ge \ tirikita)^2 \quad Dha - Dha \ ge \ tirikita$$

The superscripts give the number of times that the phrase within the parentheses is to be played or recited.

Variation II

$$+ \quad (Dha \ ge \ tirikita \ Dha \ -)^3 \quad Ta - Dha \ ge \ tirikita$$
$$o \quad (Ta \ ke \ tirikita \ Ta \ -)^2$$
$$\quad Dha \ ge \ tirikita \ Dha - \quad Dha - Dha \ ge \ tirikita$$

Lesson 3.2.   First Kaida: Variation II

+	Dha ge	ti ri	ki ta	Dha -	Dha ge	ti ri	ki ta	Dha -
o	Dha ge	ti ri	ki ta	Dha -	Ta -	Dha ge	ti ri	ki ta
+	Ta ke	ti ri	ki ta	Ta -	Ta ke	ti ri	ki ta	Ta -
o	Dha ge	ti ri	ki ta	Dha -	Dha -	Dha ge	ti ri	ki ta

Practice sequence

Theka: 1 cycle at 1 beat per second
Theme: 1 time at 2 strokes per beat
Variations: 1 time each at 4 strokes per beat

In the second variation, the initial phrase drawn from the theme is longer than in the previous variation. Thus the initial phrase from Variation I is included in the initial phrase in Variation II. Once a phrase is introduced in a variation, it is likely to recur in a subsequent variation.

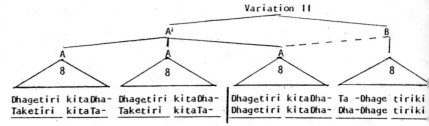

Variation II

+ Dhagetiri kitaDha- Dhagetiri kitaDha- Dhagetiri kitaDha- Ta -Dhage tiriki
o Taketiri kitaTa- Taketiri kitaTa- Dhagetiri kitaDha- Dha-Dhage tiriki

The broken line is meant to show the inherent structural ambiguity of Variation II. Note that Variation II ends with (AB), a restatement of the theme. Thus it is equally accurate to express the structure either as (AAA)(B) or as (AA)(AB). You can think of the third A-phrase as serving both functions at once. Such structural ambiguities are a delight to the connoisseur and a headache to the novice.

Variation III

+ (Dha ge tirikita Dha)^3 - Ta - Dha - Dha ge tirikita

o (Ta ke tirikita Ta)^2
 └→Dha
 Dha ge tirikita Dha - Dha - Dha - Dha ge tirikita

The arrow means "on the last repetition of the phrase within parentheses, say the syllable at the tail of the arrow and escape." This notation is equivalent to

o Ta ke tirikita Ta
 Ta ke tirikita Dha
 Dha ge tirikita Dha - Dha - Dha ge tirikita

Lesson 3.3   First Kaida: Variation III

+   Dha ge ti ri ki ta Dha,Dha ge ti ri ki ta Dha,Dha ge

o   ti ri ki ta Dha - Ta - Dha - Dha ge ti ri ki ta

+   Ta ke ti ri ki ta Ta, Ta ke ti ri ki ta Dha,Dha ge

o   ti ri ki ta Dha - Dha - Dha - Dha ge ti ri ki ta

Practice sequence:
Theka: 1 cycle at 1 beat per second
Theme: 1 time at 2 strokes per beat
Theme: 2 times at 4 strokes per beat
Variations: 1 time each at 4 strokes per beat

Variation III is a little tricky: the 7-stroke phrase Dha ge tirikita
Dha sometimes begins out of phase with the beat. Generally the succeeding
variations of a kaida elaboration become increasingly complex, as in
this case.

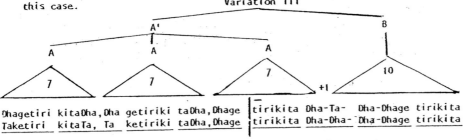

Variation III

Variation IV

+   (Dha ge tirikita Dha Dha Dha)^3 Ta - Dha - tirikita

o   (Ta ke tirikita Ta Ta Ta)^2
        ↳Dha Dha Dha
    Dha ge tirikita Dha - Dha - tirikita

Lesson 3.4   First Kaida: Variation IV

+	Dha ge ti ri	ki ta	Dha Dha	Dha,Dha ge ti	ri ki	ta Dha
o	Dha Dha,Dha ge	ti ri	ki ta	Ta - Dha -	ti ri	ki ta
+	Ta ke ti ri	ki ta	Ta Ta	Ta, Ta ke ti	ri ki	ta Dha
o	Dha Dha,Dha ge	ti ri	ki ta	Dha - Dha -	ti ri	ki ta

Practice sequence
Theka: 1 cycle at 1 beat per second
Theme: 1 time at 2 strokes per beat
Theme: 2 times at 4 strokes per beat
Variations: 1 time each at 4 strokes per beat

A 9-syllable phrase begins variation IV. The four Dha's in a row and
the ge which follows have the intonation contour low-high-high-high-low.

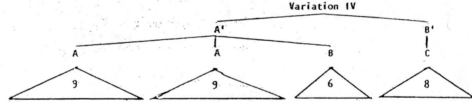

Notice the absence of ge in the B'-phrase.

Variation V

+   Dha ge tirikita (Dha Dha - Dha)^2 Dha Dha
     Dha ge tirikita Dha - Ta - Dha ge tirikita

o   Ta ke tirikita (Ta Ta - Ta)^2
                          ↳Dha Dha Dha
     Dha ge tirikita Dha - Dha - Dha ge tirikita

Lesson 3.5   First kaida: Variation V

+	Dha ge	ti ri	ki ta	Dha Dha	- 9ha	Dha Dha - Dha	Dha Dha
o	Dha ge	ti ri	ki ta	Dha -	Ta -	Dha ge ti ri	ki ta
+	Ta ke	ti ri	ki ta	Ta Ta	- Ta	Ta Ta - Dha	Dha Dha
o	Dha ge	ti ri	ki ta	Dha -	Dha -	Dha ge ti ri	ki ta

Practice sequence
  Theka: 1 cycle at 1 beat per second
  Theme: 1 time at 2 strokes per beat
  Theme: 2 times at 4 strokes per beat
  Variations: 1 each at 4 strokes per beat

Variation V has a simple structure, a 16-stroke phrase followed by a
a restatement of the theme. This variation illustrates the use of the
rest.

Variation V

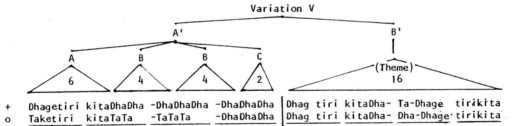

| + | Dhagetiri | kitaDhaDha | -DhaDhaDha | -DhaDhaDha | Dhag tiri kitaDha- Ta-Dhage tirikita |
| o | Taketiri | kitaTaTa | -TaTaTa | -DhaDhaDha | Dhag tiri kitaDha- Dha-Dhage tirikita |

Variation VI

+ $(\text{Dha ge tirikita } (\text{Dha Dha - Dha})^2 \text{ Dha Dha})^3$
  Dha ge tirikita Dha - Ta - Dha ge tirikita

o $(\text{Ta ke tirikita } (\text{Ta Ta - Ta})^2 \text{ Ta Ta})^2$
       ↳Dha Dha₂Dha
  Dha ge tirikita $(\text{Dha Dha - Dha})^2$ Dha Dha
  Dha ge tirikita Dha - Dha - Dha ge tirikita

(Note: when parentheses occur within parentheses, expand the inner parentheses first.)

Lesson 3.6 First kaida: Variation VI

+	Dha ge	ti ri	ki ta	Dha Dha	- Dha	Dha Dha	- Dha	Dha Dha
o	Dha ge	ti ri	ki ta	Dha Dha	- Dha	Dha Dha	- Dha	Dha Dha
+	Dha ge	ti ri	ki ta	Dha Dha	- Dha	Dha Dha	- Dha	Dha Dha
o	Dha ge	ti ri	ki ta	Dha -	Ta -	Dha ge	ti ri	ki ta
+	Ta ke	ti ri	ki ta	Ta Ta	- Ta	Ta Ta	- Ta	Ta Ta
o	Ta ke	ti ri	ki ta	Ta Ta	- Ta	Ta Ta	- Dha	Dha Dha
+	Dha ge	ti ri	ki ta	Dha Dha	- Dha	Dha Dha	- Dha	Dha Dha
-	Dha ge	ti ri	ki ta	Dha -	Dha -	Dha ge	ti ri	ki ta

Practice sequence
Theka: 1 cycle at 1 beat per second
Theme: 1 time at 2 strokes per beat
Theme: 2 times at 4 strokes per beat
Variations: 1 time each at 4 strokes per beat

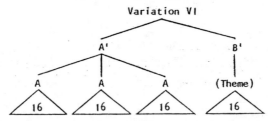

where A = Dhagetirikita (DhaDha-Dha)^2 DhaDha, or A' from Variation V, and

B = DhagetirikitaDha- Ta-Dhagetirikita, the Kaida Theme.

Variations II and VI are formed in a similar manner -- by doubling of a previously introduced phrase.

Variation VII

+ (DhaDhaDhaDha Dhagetirikita)^2 Dha-Ta-Dha-Dhagetirikita

o TaTaTaTa Taketirikita
DhaDhaDhaDha Dhagetirikita Dha-Dha-Dha-Dhagetirikita

Lesson 3.7   First Kaida: Variation VII

+	Dha Dha	Dha Dha	Dha ge	ti ri	ki ta	Dna Dha	Dha Dha	Dha ge
o	ti ri	ki ta	Dha -	Ta -	Dha -	Dha ge	ti ri	ki ta
+	Ta Ta	Ta Ta	Ta ke	ti ri	ki ta	Dha Dha	Dha Dha	Dha ge
o	ti ri	ki ta	Dha -	Dha -	Dha -	Dha ge	ti ri	ki ta

Practice sequence
                  Theka: 1 cycle at 1 beat per second
                  Theme: 1 time at 2 strokes per beat
                  Theme: 2 times at 4 strokes per beat
                  Variations: 1 time each at 4 strokes per beat

Variation VII takes the successive Dha's of some previous variations and Places them at the beginning of the phrase. The 5 Dha's and the ge have the intonation contour high-high-high-high-high-low.

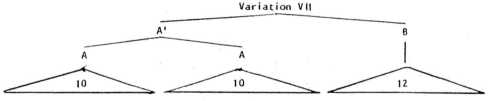

Variation VII completes the sequence of variations on the Kaida Theme.

Tihai

A tihai is a rhythmic structure in which a phrase ending in Dha is played or recited 3 times. Usually the final Dha falls on the sam and concludes the composition.

Tihai

$$((Dha \text{ ge tirikita } Dha)^3 -)^3$$
$$+$$

When parentheses occur within other parentheses, expand the inner-most parentheses first. The above notation is equivalent to

(Dha ge tirikita Dha   3 x (7 strokes
Dha ge tirikita Dha   =   7   "
Dha ge tirikita Dha -)³   7   "   + 1 stroke)
              +   =   3 x 22 strokes

                           =   66 strokes

At 4 strokes per beat, 66 strokes spans 16 beats (or 1 cycle of tintal) plus 2 strokes. As the plus (+) under the Dha indicates, the final Dha (the 65th stroke) falls on a sam. The final stroke is a rest (-).

Lesson 3.8   First Kaida: Tihai

+ Dha ge ti ri   ki ta   Dha,Dha | ge ti   ri ki   ta Dha, Dha ge

o ti ri   ki ta   Dha -; Dha ge | ti ri   ki ta   Dha,Dha ge ti

+ ri ki   ta Dha, Dha ge ti ri | ki ta   Dha -;   Dha ge   ti ri

o ki ta   Dha,Dha ge ti   ri ki | ta Dha, Dha ge   ti ri   ki ta

+ Dha

   -The semicolon (;) has no time value; it shows the boundary
   between the three parts of the tihai.

   Practice sequence
         Theka: 1 cycle at 1 beat per second
         Theme: 1 time at 2 strokes per beat
         Theme: 2 times at 4 strokes per beat
         Variations: 1 time each at 4 strokes per beat
         Tihai: 1 time at 4 strokes per beat.

This tihai is special in that each of its three equal sections is itself a tihai.

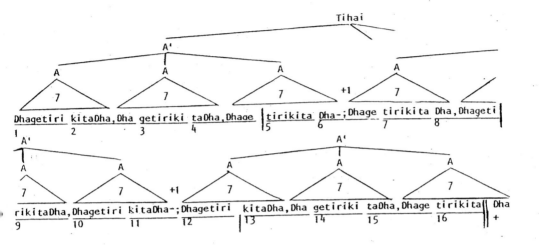

Chakradar tihai

$$((\text{Dha ge tirikita Dha Dha Dha})^3 \qquad 3 \times (24 \text{ strokes}$$
$$\quad \longrightarrow \text{Dha ti Dha} - - \text{K't})^3 \qquad +16 \text{ strokes})$$
$$\qquad \longrightarrow - - - - -)^3 \quad +(2 \times 5 \text{ strokes})$$
$$= 130 \text{ strokes}$$

The bol K't sounds like the English word "cut."

At 4 strokes per beat the chakradar tihai spans 2 cycles of tintal, with the final Dha falling on sam.

Lesson 3.9   First Kaida: Chakradar tihai

+	Dha ge	ti ri	ki ta	Dha Dha	Dha,Dha	ge ti	ri ki	ta Dha
o	Dha Dha,Dha ge	ti ri	ki ta	Dha ti	Dha -	- K't	Dha ti
+	Dha -	- K't	Dha ti	Dha -,	(1)(2)	(3)(4)	(5)Dha	ge ti
o	rI ki	ta Dha	Dha Dha,Dha ge	ti ri	ki ta	Dha Dha Dha,Dha
+	ge ti	ri ki	ta Dha	ti Dha	- -	K't Dha ti Dha	- -
o	K't Dha ti Dha	-,(1)	(2)(3)	(4)(5)		Dha ge	ti ri	ki ta
+	Dha Dha Dha,Dha	ge ti	ri ki	ta Dha	Dha Dha,Dha ge	ti ri
o	ki ta	Dha ti	Dha -	- K't	Dha ti	Dha -	- K't	Dha ti
+	Dha							

- The symbol Dha is played "sur Dha" and is pronounced "Dhā" in the usual manner.

- Count the rests 1 through 5 aloud when practicing reciting or playing, but not when performing.

Practice sequence

    Theka: 1 cycle at 1 beat per second
    Theme: 1 time at 2 strokes per beat
    Theme: 2 strokes at 4 strokes per beat
    Variations: 1 time each at 4 strokes per beat
    Chakradar tihai: 1 time at 4 strokes per beat

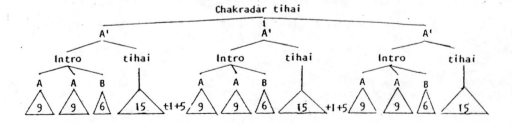

Chakradar tihai

where A = Dha ge tirikita Dha Dha Dha, B = Dha ge tirikita

and the tihai = (Dha ti Dha - - K't)

ach of the 3 main limbs of the chakradar tihai is composed of an introductory phrase (from Variation IV) plus a short tihai. The word "chakradar" comes from the Hindi term for "wheel"; indeed the chakradar tihai is aptly described as "wheels within wheels."

Although Khan-Sahab teaches two tihais with this kaida elaboration, only one should be played or recited at the end of the sequence of variations.

In conducting class, Alla Rakha has his students follow these practice procedures:

1. Keep tal when reciting.

2. Memorize each lesson thoroughly at the practice tempo -- 1 beat per second. Strive for clear, consistent tone and pronunciation. Then, increase the tempo to 2 beats per second, the speed of the compositions as demonstrated on the accompanying tape cassette.

3. Play in context. Specifically:

   a. Begin each lesson or exercise with a cycle of theka.

   b. Make up practice sequences, such as the following:

   Theka: 1 cycle at 2 beats per second.
   Kaida theme: Recite 1 time at 2 syllables per beat.
      "   "   Play 1 time at 2 strokes per beat.
      "   "   : Recite 2 times at 4 syllables per beat.
      "   "   : Play 2 times at 4 strokes per beat.
   Each variation: Recite 1 time at 4 syllables per beat
      "   "   : Play 3 times at 4 strokes per beat/
      tihai: Recite 1 time at 4 syllables per beat.
      "   : Play 1 time at 4 syllables per beat.
      -Return to the theka and repeat the sequence.

See Chapter Eight for a discussion of the conventions for the performance of tabla solos.

46

INTERCHAPTER C

New Strokes for the Second Kaida

The second kaida features the bol tita (also written tit), which is two dry taps on the center of the dayan

1) From the starting position, rotate the forearm to strike ti with the cushion of the index finger on the center of the shyahi.

2) Rotate the forearm back to the starting position to strike ta with the cushion of the middle finger on the center of the shyahi.

This way of playing tita, with the index finger first, is distinctive of Alla Rakha's style. Khan-Sahab also teaches the more common way of playing tita, with the middle finger first, as in the Peshkar and in the fixed composition known as the Chakradar Gat.

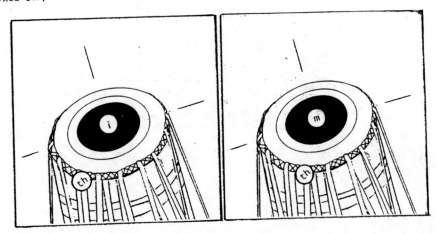

Exercise CI   gi na ti ta
                 i   i   m

||: gi na ti ta - - :||

Exercise C2   gi na ti ta Dha ge na
                 i   i   m   i   m

||: gi na ti ta Dha ge na - :||

-"gi" is another name for "ge."

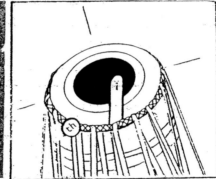

tin can be played "open," as a stroke of the full index finger alone on the axis of the tabla. The drum is permitted to ring its full sound, unlike tin in the theka, in which the sound is partially dampened by the outer fingers. As in the theka, this tin is accompanied by a ka on the bayan, played with the knuckles.

Exercise C3   tin na gi na
                         m

||: tin na ge na :||

Exercise C4   Dha ti Dha ge na, tin na gi na
                 i   m   i   m   m

||: - Dha |ti Dha ge na tin na ge na :||

- Remember to play tin with ka on the bayan.

Exercise C5 gi na ti ta Dha ge na, Dha ti Dha ge na tin na gi na

gi na ti ta Dha ge na,Dha | ti Dha ge na tin na gi na

-This is the Second Kaida Theme from sam to khali.

Exercise C6 ki na ti ta Ta ke na, Dha ti Dha ge na dhin na ge na

ki na ti ta Ta ke na,Dha | ti Dha ge na dhinna gi na

-This is the theme from khali to sam.

-ki and ke are played the same, with the open hand.

At this point you can turn to Chapter Four and learn the Second Kaida through Variation V.

The following phrase occurs in Variation VI.

Exercise C7 ti ta Ta ti ta ti ta

||: - ti ta Ta ti ta ti ta, | ti ta Ta ti ta ti ta - :||

-Ta is played "sur Ta," as described in Interchapter B.

This next phrase occurs in the chakradar tihai.

Exercise C8 (Dha - ti - Dha - Ta - Ta)^3

Dha - ti - Dha - Ta - | Ta,Dha - ti - Dha - Ta

- Ta Dha - ti - Dha -

-The Ta's are optional. Most students find the version with the Ta's a little easier.

C H A P T E R   F O U R

Second Kaida: gina tita Dhagena...

Most kaida themes end with a distinctive B-phrase which features
the bol <u>tin</u> or <u>dhin</u>; the second kaida is a good example. In the variations
of the second kaida, Alla Rakha introduces permutation, a powerful tool
in rhythmic improvisation.

Theme: +   gina tita Dhagena, DhatiDhagena tinnagina
          o   kina tita Takena, DhatiDhagena dhinnagina

Lesson 4.0 Second Kaida: Theme

-Recite and keep tal, or play on the drums, at the slow tempo,
one beat per second.

+   <u>gi na</u>   <u>ti ta</u>   <u>Dha ge na</u>,Dha | <u>ti Dha ge na</u>   <u>tin na gi na</u>

o   <u>ki na</u>   <u>ti ta</u> '<u>Ta ke na</u>,Dha | <u>ti Dha ge na</u>   <u>dhinna gi na</u>

-Practice sequence
               Theka: 1 cycle at 1 stroke per beat
               Theme: 1 time at 2 strokes per beat
               "   : 2 times at 4 strokes per beat

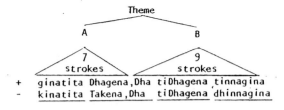

Theme
       A   B
      7   9
   strokes   strokes

+   <u>ginatita</u> <u>Dhagena</u>,Dha <u>tiDhagena</u> <u>tinnagina</u>
−   <u>kinatita</u> <u>Takena</u>,Dha <u>tiDhagena</u> <u>dhinnagina</u>

Variation I: +   (gina tita Dhagena)^2
                     gina tita tita Dhagena DhatiDhagena tinnagina

          o   (kina tita Takena)^2
                     gina dhita dhita Dhagena DhatiDhagena dhinnagina

---

Lesson 4. I Second kaida: Variation I

-Slow tintal -- I beat per second

+ gi na ti ta Dha ge na,gi | na ti ta Dha ge na, gi na

o ti ta ti ta Dha ge na,Dha | ti Dha ge na tin na gi na

+ ki na ti ta Ta ke na,ki | na ti ta Ta ke na, gi na

o dhi ta dhi ta Dha ge na,Dha | ti Dha ge na dhinna gi na

Practice sequence

              Theka: I cycle at I stroke per beat
            Theme: I time at 2 strokes per beat
               " : 2 times at 4 strokes per beat
      Variations: I time at 4 strokes per beat

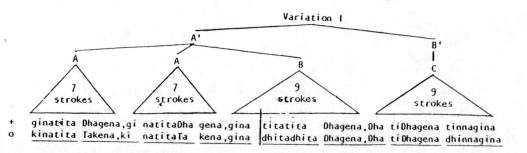

Variation I

+ ginatita Dhagena,gi natitaDha gena,gina titatita Dhagena,Dha tiDhagena tinnagina
o kinatita Takena,ki natitaTa kena,gina dhitadhita Dhagena,Dha tiDhagena dhinnagina

Variation II: + (gina tita tita Dhagena)^2
                  tita Dhagena DhatiDhagena tinnagina

        o (kina tita tita Takena)^2
                  dhita Dhagena DhatiDhagena dhinnagina

Lesson 4.2 Second Kaida: Variation II

-Slow tintal -- 1 beat per second

+	gi na	ti ta	ti ta	Dha ge	na, gi	na ti	ta ti	ta Dha
o	ge na,	ti ta	Dha ge	na,Dha	ti Dha	ge na	tin na	gi na
+	ki na	ti ta	ti ta	Ta ke	na,ki	na ti	ta ti	ta, Ta
o	ke na,	dhi ta	Dha ge	na,Dha	ti Dha	ge na	dhinna	gi na

Practice sequence
Theka: 1 cycle at 1 stroke per beat
Theme: 1 cycle at 2 strokes per beat
     " : 2 times at 4 strokes per beat
Variations: 1 time each at 4 strokes per beat

Variation II begins with the 9-stroke phrase introduced in

Variation I.

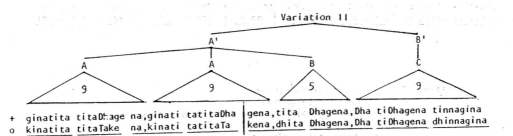

Variation II

A'
A   A   B
9   9   5   B' C 9

+ ginatita titaDhage na,ginati tatitaDha | gena,tita Dhagena,Dha tiDhagena tinnagina
o kinatita titaTake na,kinati tatitaTa | kena,dhita Dhagena,Dha tiDhagena dhinnagina

Variation III: + gina (tita)^3 Dhagena
                  (tita)^2 Dhagena
                  tita Dhagena DhatiDhagena tinnagina

          o kina (tita)^3 Takena
                  (tita)^2 Takena
                  dhita Dhagena DhatiDhagena dhinnagina

Lesson 4.3 Second kaida: Variation III

| + | gi na | ti ta | ti ta | ti ta | Dha ge na,ti | ta ti | ta,Dha |
| o | ge na | ti ta | Dha ge na,Dha | ti Dha ge na | tin na gi na |

| + | ki na | ti ta | ti ta | ti ta | Ta ke na,ti | ta ti | ta Ta |
| o | ke na, dhi ta | Dha ge na,Dha | ti Dha ge na | dhinna gi na |

Practice sequence: as the previous variations

Variation III

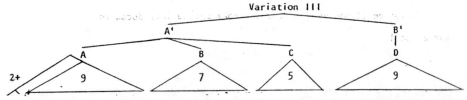

  + ginatita titatita Dhagena,ti tatitaDha |gena,tita Dhagena,Dha ti Dhagena tinnagina
  o kinatita titatita Takena,ti tatitaTa |kena,dhita Dhagena,Dha ti Dhagena dhinnagina

---

Variation IV: + gina (tita)^3 Dhagena
                  tita Dhagena
                  (tita)^2 Dhagena DhatiDhagena tinnagina

          o kina (tita)^3 Takena
                  tita Takena
                  (dhita)^2 Dhagena DhatiDhagena dhinnagina

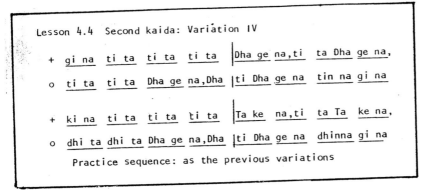

Lesson 4.4 Second kaida: Variation IV

+ <u>gi na</u> <u>ti ta</u> <u>ti ta</u> <u>ti ta</u> | <u>Dha ge na</u>,<u>ti</u> <u>ta Dha ge na</u>,

o <u>ti ta</u> <u>ti ta</u> <u>Dha ge na</u>,<u>Dha</u> | <u>ti Dha ge na</u> <u>tin na gi na</u>

+ <u>ki na</u> <u>ti ta</u> <u>ti ta</u> <u>ti ta</u> | <u>Ta ke na</u>,<u>ti</u> <u>ta Ta ke na</u>,

o <u>dhi ta</u> <u>dhi ta</u> <u>Dha ge na</u>,<u>Dha</u> | <u>ti Dha ge na</u> <u>dhinna gi na</u>

Practice sequence: as the previous variations

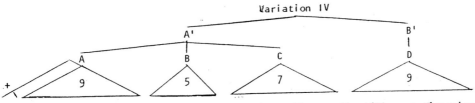

Variation IV

+ <u>ginatita titatita Dhagena</u>,<u>ti taDhagena</u>,|<u>titatita</u> <u>Dhagena</u>,<u>Dha tiDhagena tinnagina</u>
o <u>kinatita titatita Takena</u>,<u>ti taTakena</u>, |<u>dhitadhita Dhagena</u>,<u>Dha tiDhagena dhinnagina</u>

Did you notice that this variation is a re-ordering of the groups in the

A'-phrase of the previous variation? Since 9 strokes plus 7 strokes plus 5 strokes

will always equal 21 strokes not matter in what order they are played, then every

possible reordering of these phrases will be a permissible variation on the

kaida theme for tintal. A re-ordering of phrases within a kaida variation

is usually called a "permutation." There are six permutations of the phrases:

As the table shows, only two of the permutations actually occur in this particular kaida development. The remaining permutations can be used in other developments on this theme. Tabla players sometimes practice playing or reciting all possible permutations in order, as an excercise.

Variation V: + gina $((tita)^2$ Dhagena$)^3$ DhatiDhagena tinnagina

    o kina $((tita)^2{}_2$Takena$)^2$
      $(dhita)^2$ Dhagena DhatiDhagena dhinnagina

Lesson 4.5 Second kaida: Variation V

+ gi na ti ta ti ta Dha ge |na,ti ta ti ta Dha ge na,

o ti ta ti ta Dha ge na,Dha |ti Dha ge na tin na gi na

+ ki na ti ta ti ta Ta ke |na,ti ta ti ta Ta ke na,

o dhi ta dhi ta Dha ge na,Dha |ti Dha ge na dhinna gi na

Practice sequence: as the previous variations

Variation V

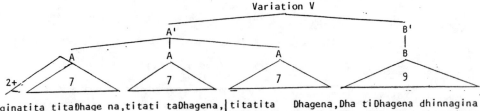

+ ginatita titaDhage na,titati taDhagena, titatita Dhagena,Dha tiDhagena dhinnagina
o kinatita titaTake na,titati taTakena, dhitadhita Dhagena,Dha tiDhagena tinnagina

Strictly speaking, Variation V is not a mere permutation of Variations III and IV. These variations are all members of a family of variations defined by a formula:

  + gina $(tita)^a$ Dhagena
    $(tita)^b$ "
    $(tita)^c$ " DhatiDhagena tinnagina
 o ...

The superscripts a, b, and c indicate the number of times that tita is
to be played. For the formula to generate only tintal phrases we must
further specify that

$$a + b + c = 6.$$

For Variation III, for instance, a = 3, b = 2, and c = 1. For Variation V,
a = b = c = 2.

Variation VI: + gina (tita)^2 Dhagena (tita$\overset{*}{T}$atitatita)^2 DhatiDhagena tinnagina

         o kina (tita)^2 Takena tita$\overset{*}{T}$atitatita

                     dhitaDhadhitadhita DhatiDhagena dhinnagina

Note: The bol $\overset{*}{T}a$ is played "sur Ta" on the tabla, and is pronounced
simply "Tā" during recitation.

Lesson 4.6   Second kaida: Variation VI

+ gi na ti ta   ti ta Dha ge |na,ti ta $\overset{*}{Ta}$ ti ta   ti ta,

o ti ta $\overset{*}{Ta}$ ti ta ti ta,Dha |ti Dha ge na tin na gi na

+ ki na ti ta   ti ta Ta ke |na,ti ta $\overset{*}{Ta}$ ti ta   ti ta,

o dhi ta $\overset{*}{Dhadhi}$ ta dhi ta Dha ,ti Dha ge na dhinna gi na

Practice sequence: as the previous variations

In this variation Khan-Sahab bends the rules a bit by introducing
the stroke sur Tā (symbolized T$\overset{*}{a}$), which does not occur in the theme.
Sur Ta often occurs in the tihai which concludes the kaida development;
the sur Ta in variation VI foreshadows the tihai, which follows immediately.

Variation VI

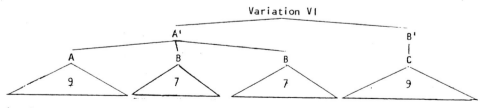

ginatita titaDhage na,titaTa titatita,|titaTati tatita,Dha tiDhagena tinnagina
kinatita titaTake na,titaTa titatita,|dhitaDhadhi tadhita,Dha tiDhagena dhinnagina

Chakradar tihai + (gina tita Dhagena, DhatiDhagena tinnagina

(Dha-ti-Dha-, *Ta-*Ta)^3
+
↳ - - - - -)^3

Note: the sur Ta's are optional, and may be replaced by pauses (-). Most students find it easier to learn the chakradar by including the sur Ta's.

Lesson 4.7 Second kaida: The Chakradar tihai

+	gi na	ti ta	Dha ge	na, Dha	ti Dha	ge na	tin na	gi na
o	Dha -	ti -	Dha -,	*Ta -	*Ta, Dha	- ti	- Dha	-, *Ta
+	- *Ta,	Dha -	ti -	Dha -,	(1)(2)	(3)(4)	(5);gi	na ti
o	ta Dha	ge na,	Dha ti	Dha ge	na tin	na gi	na Dha	- ti
+	- Dha	- *Ta	- *Ta,	Dha -	ti -	Dha -	*Ta -	*Ta, Dha
o	- ti	- Dha	-, (1)	(2)(3)	(4)(5)	gi na	ti ta	Dha ge
+	na, Dha	ti Dha	ge na	tin na	gi na	Dha -	ti -	Dha -
o	*Ta -	*Ta, Dha	- ti	- Dha	-, *Ta	- *Ta	Dha -	ti -
	Dha							

- As in the chakradar to the first kaida, count the rests 1 to 5 aloud when practicing reciting or playing, but not when performing.

Practice sequence

Theka: 1 time at 1 stroke per beat
Theme: 1 time at 2 strokes per beat
" 2 times at 4 strokes per beat
Variations: 1 time each at 4 strokes per beat
Chakradar tihai: 1 time at 4 strokes per beat

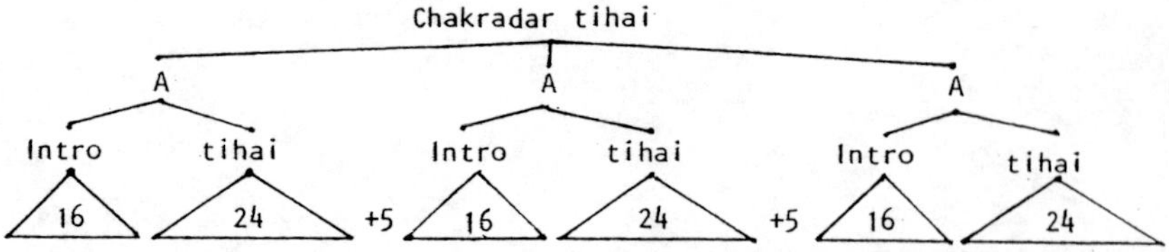

where Intro = ginatita Dhagena, DhatiDhagena tinnagina (Kaida Theme)

and tihai = (Dha-ti-Dha-, Ta-Ta)^3
+

INTERCHAPTER D

New Stroke for the Peshkar

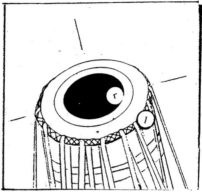

d̤ is a dry, unstressed tap of the ring finger on the edge of the shyahi. The bol is pronounced retroflex (tongue touching the roof of the mouth) and slightly "r-colored." The ligature over the letter and the rest (-d̂) indicates that the two symbols together represent a duration of one syllable. In the Peshkar, Dha is always played sur Dha.

Here are the phrases of the theme:

Exercise D1   Dha -d Dha tin na

‖: Dha -d̂ Dhatin na - :‖

-Remember to play a ka on the bayan each time you strike tin.

Exercise D2   Dha -d Dha ti ta ka

‖: - Dha -d̂ Dha ti ta ka - :‖

Exercise D3   Dha -d Dha tin na, Dha -d Dha ti ta ka, Dha -d Dha tin na

-This is the Peshkar Theme, from sam to khali.

Dha -d̂ Dhatin na, Dha -d̂ Dha | ti ta ka, Dha -d̂ Dha tin na

58

Exercise D4 Ta -d Ta tin na, Dha -d Dha ti ta ka, Dha -d Dha dhin na

-This is the theme from khali to sam.

Ta -d Ta tin na,Dha -d Dha |ti ta ka,Dha -d Dha dhinna

You can now turn to Chapter Five and learn the Peshkar Theme and the first three variations.

The following phrase occurs in Variation IV

Exercise D5 Dha -d, Dha -d Dha tin na

|| : Dha -d Dha -d Dhatin na - : ||

CHAPTER FIVE

Peshkar

The peshkar follows the theka at the beginning of the tabla solo. The peshkar is a theme and variation form which features bols of the theka (such as Dha, dhin, tin, etc.) appearing in new and surprising patterns.

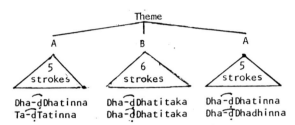

The ligature above the rest and the bol (⁀d) means that they have a combined duration equal to a single stroke or syllable.

The sound ḍ does not occur as such in American English. After pronouncing Dha curl the tongue back (this position is called "retroflex") to create an r-like sound, and then pronounce a d against the alveolar ridge (the ridge behind the teeth).

Lesson 5.0   Peshkar: Theme

Recite and keep tal, or play on the drums, at the practice tempo: 1 beat per second.

+   Dha ⁀d Dhatin na, Dha ⁀d Dha | ti ta ka, Dha ⁀d Dha · tin na

o   Ta ⁀d Ta tin na, Dha ⁀d Dha | ti ta ka, Dha ⁀d Dha dhinna

Practice sequence
Theka: 1 time at 1 stroke per beat
Theme: 2 times at 2 strokes per beat
*Dha and Ta are played sur Dha and sur Ta throughout the peshkar.

60

Each line of the theme has the structure ABA, where A is the 5-stroke
phrase Dha-dDhatinna and B is the 6-stroke phrase Dha-dDhatitaka.
As in the kaidas, Dha is played Ta at khali, and tin becomes dhin when
approaching sam.

Once each lesson has been memorized, it should be practiced at the
performance tempo, 2 beats per second.

Variation I: + (Dha-dDhatinna)^2 Dha-dDhatitaka
              o   Dha-dDhatinna Dha-dDhatitaka Dha-dDhatinna

              + (Ta-dTatinna)^2 Dha-dDhatitaka
              o   Dha-dDhatinna Dha-dDhatitaka Dha-dDhadhinna

---

Lesson 5.1 Peshkar: Variation I

+ Dha -d Dhatin na, Dha -d. Dha |tin na Dha -d Dha-ti ta ka

o Dha -d Dhatin na, Dha -d. Dha |ti ta ka, Dha -d. Dha tin na

+ Ta -d Ta tin na, Ta -d Ta |tin na Dha -d Dha ti ta ka

o Dha -d Dhatin na, Dha -d:Dha |ti ta ka, Dha -d. Dha dhinna

-Practice sequence
                     Theka: 1 cycle at 1 stroke per beat
                     Theme: 1 time at 2 strokes per beat
              Variation I: 2 times at 2 strokes per beat

Variation I

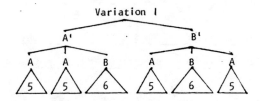

where A → Dha-dDhatinna

and B = Dha-dDhatitaka

The first variation is generated in a familiar way, by doubling the first phrase from the theme, and then playing the B-phrase.(AAB). The rest of the variation consists of a restatement of the theme (ABA), giving each cycle (avartan) of Variation I the structure (AAB)(ABA).

Variation II: + (Dha-ḍDhatinna Dha-ḍDhatita)² Dha-ḍDhatitakata Dha-ḍDhatinna
              o Ta-ḍTatinna Ta-ḍTatita
                 Dha-ḍDhatinna Dha-ḍDhatita Dha-ḍDhatitakata Dha-ḍDhadhinna

---

Lesson 5.2   Peshkar: Variation II

+ Dha -d Dhatin na, Dha -d Dha | ti ta, Dha -d Dhatin na, Dha

o -d Dha ti ta, Dha -d Dha ti | ta ka ta, Dha -d Dha tin na

+ Ta -d Ta tin na, Ta -d Ta | ti ta, Dha -d Dhatin na, Dha

o -d Dha ti ta, Dha -d Dha ti | ta ka ta, Dha -d Dha dhinna

-Practice sequence
              Theka: 1 cycle at 1 stroke per beat
             Theme: 1 time at 2 strokes per beat
      Variations: 2 times each at 2 strokes per beat

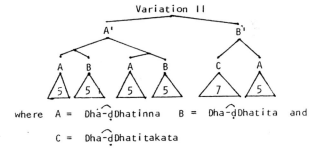

Variation II

where A = Dha-ḍDhatinna   B = Dha-ḍDhatita and

C = Dha-ḍDhatitakata

This variation begins like the first variation, with a doubled phrase from the theme (AB)(AB). Each cycle of Variation II has the structure (AB)(AB)C A.

Variation III: +   (Dha-d̂Dhatinna)³ Dha-d̂Dhatita Dha-d̂Dhatitakata
Dha-d̂Dhatinna

o   (Ta-d̂Tatinna)²
Dha-d̂Dhatinna Dha-d̂Dhatita Dha-d̂Dhatitakata
Dha-d̂Dhadhinna

Lesson 5.3 Peshkar: Variation III

+ Dha -d̂ Dhatin na, Dha -d̂ Dha │tin na, Dha -d̂ Dhatin na, Dha

o -d̂ Dha ti ta Dha -d̂ Dha ti │ta ka ta, Dha -d̂ Dha tin na

+ Ta -d̂ Ta tin na, Ta -d̂ Ta │tin na, Dha -d̂ Dhatin na, Dha

o -d̂ Dha ti ta Dha -d̂ Dha ti │ta ka ta, Dha -d̂ Dha dhinna

-Practice sequence: as the previous variation

Variation III

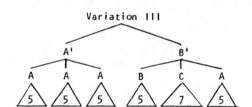

where A = Dha-d̂Dhatinna,   B = Dha-d̂Dhatita,   and   C = Dha-d̂Dhatitakata

Whereas the first rwo variations began with a phrase from the theme which
was doubled, the third variations begins with a phrase played three times.

Variation IV: + $(Dha\widehat{-d}Dha\widehat{-d}Dhatinna)^3$ $Dha\widehat{-d}Dhatitaka$
$Dha\widehat{-d}Dhatinna$

+ $(Ta\widehat{-d}Ta\widehat{-d}Tatinna)^2$ $Dha\widehat{-d}Dha\widehat{-d}Dhatinna$ $Dha\widehat{-d}Dhatitaka$
$Dha\widehat{-d}Dhadhinna$

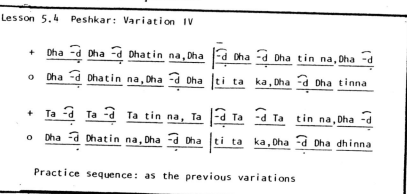

Lesson 5.4   Peshkar: Variation IV

+   Dha $\widehat{-d}$ Dha $\widehat{-d}$ Dhatin na,Dha | $\overline{-d}$ Dha $\widehat{-d}$ Dha tin na,Dha $\widehat{-d}$

o   Dha $\widehat{-d}$ Dhatin na,Dha $\widehat{-d}$ Dha | ti ta ka,Dha $\widehat{-d}$ Dha tinna

+   Ta $\widehat{-d}$ Ta $\widehat{-d}$ Ta tin na, Ta | $\overline{-d}$ Ta $\overline{-d}$ Ta tin na,Dha $\widehat{-d}$

o   Dha $\widehat{-d}$ Dhatin na,Dha $\widehat{-d}$ Dha | ti ta ka,Dha $\widehat{-d}$ Dha dhinna

Practice sequence: as the previous variations

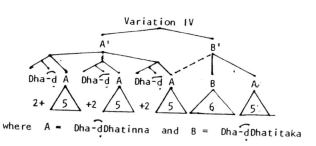

where A = Dha$\widehat{-d}$Dhatinna and B = Dha$\widehat{-d}$Dhatitaka

Here is another example of an ambiguous structure. The third A-phrase of the variation has a double function. The dotted line shows that it may be thought of as part of a restatement of the theme, ABA. Alternatively the third A-phrase may be thought of as part of an initial phrase which is played 3 times, as in the preceding variation.

Tihai: $((\text{Dha-}\overset{\frown}{\text{d}}\text{Dhatinna})^{4}\ \text{Dha -})^{3}$
+

Lesson 5.5 Peshkar: tihai

+ Dha $\overset{\frown}{\text{-d}}$ Dhatin na,Dha $\overset{\frown}{\text{-d}}$ Dha │tin na,Dha $\overset{\frown}{\text{-d}}$ Dhatin na,Dha

o $\overset{\frown}{\text{-d}}$ Dha tin na Dha -; Dha $\overset{\frown}{\text{-d}}$ │Dnatin na,Dha $\overset{\frown}{\text{-d}}$ Dha tin na

+ Dha $\overset{\frown}{\text{-d}}$ Dhatin na,Dha $\overset{\frown}{\text{-d}}$ Dha │tin na Dha -; Dha $\overset{\frown}{\text{-d}}$ Dhatin

o na,Dha $\overset{\frown}{\text{-d}}$ Dha tin na Dha $\overset{\frown}{\text{-d}}$ │Dhatin na,Dha $\overset{\frown}{\text{-d}}$ Dha tin na │ Dha
                                                                                  +

Practice sequence
            Theka: 1 cycle at 1 stroke per beat
  Theme and variations: 2 times each at 2 strokes per beat
            Tihai: 1 time at 2 strokes per beat

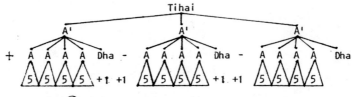

where   A = Dha-$\overset{\frown}{\text{d}}$Dhatinna

Alla Rakha here maintains his strategy of increasing the number
of repetitions of the initial phrase from one variation to the next. This
time the 5-stroke A-phrase from the theme is played 4 times, followed by Dha
as the 21st stroke. Instead of making another variation, however,
Khan-Sahab takes advantage of the fact that a 21-stroke phrase played
3 times (with a single rest between repetitions) makes a tihai in tintal.

Lesson 5.6 Peshkar: theme, variations, and tihai

    Performance sequence
                Theka: 1 time at 1 stroke per beat
                Theme: 1 time at 2 strokes per beat
           Variations: 1 time each in order at 2 strokes per beat
                Tihai 1 time at 2 strokes per beat

INTERCHAPTER E

New Stroke for the Rela

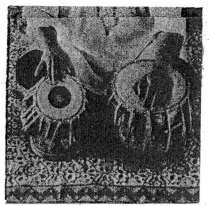 

n is a touch of the cushion of the ring finger to the kinar of the dayan. n often occurs where na might be expected.

Exercise E1   dhin $_m$ n gi $_m$ na

-dhin is played "open dhin" (That is, open tin in Exercise C3 with ge $_m$).

‖: dhin n gi na :‖

Exercise E2   ta $_{mr}$ katirikit $_r$ dhin $_m$ n gi $_m$ na

‖: ta ka ti ri ki ta dhin n gi na - - :‖

Exercise E3   Dha $_m$ - gi $_m$ dnag $_m$, ta $_{mr}$ katirikit $_r$ dhin $_m$ n gi $_m$ na

Dha - gi d na g ta ka | ti ri ki ta dhin n gi na

Exercise E4   Ta-kidnak ta $_{mr}$ ka tirikit $_r$ dhin $_m$ na gi $_m$ n

Ta - ki d na k ta ka ti ri ki ta dhin n gi na

At this point you can turn to Chapter Six and learn the Rela Theme an the first two variations.

In Variation II and subsequent variations, repetitions of the phrase takatirikit dhinngina begin with ta_i :

Exercise E5 ta_{mr}ka tirikitdhinngina, ta_ika tirikitdhinngina,
ta_i ka tirikitdhinngina

(The notation for this exercise is the same as Exercise E2.)

Similarly, in Variations III, IV, and V repetitions of takatirikita begin with the index finger, ta_i :

Exercise E6 ta_{mr} katirikita$_r$,ta_i katirikita$_r$,ta_i katirikita$_r$

$\|$: ta ka ti ri ki ta, ta ka $|$ ti ri ki ta, ta ka ti ri ki ta : $\|$

CHAPTER SIX

The Rela

The rela is the last type of theme and variation piece played in a tabla solo -- after the peshkar and kaidas. The rela is considered the "fast" theme and variation form because it is often played at 8 strokes per beat.

Theme: +   Dha-gidnag takatirikit dhinngina
             Ta-kidnak takatirikit dhinngina

In the rela we will adopt the convention of dropping the final short "a" (gidnagá, tirikitá). This allows a transliteration which is more faithful to the Devanagri script.

The bol n (pronounced "nih") is an unstressed, non-resonant tap. It often substitutes for na.

Lesson 6.0   Rela Theme

   +   Dha -   gi d   na g,   ta ka | ti ri   ki t   dhin n gi na

   -   Ta -   ki d   na k   ta ka | ti ri   ki t   dhin n gi na
       Practice sequence |
                        Theka: 1 time at 1 stroke per beat
                        Theme: 1 time at 2 strokes per beat
                         "   2 times at 4 strokes per beat

Once each lesson has been thoroughly memorized at the practice tempo of 1 beat per second, it should be learned at the performance tempo of 2 beats per second.

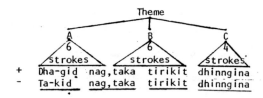

Variation I + $(\text{Dha-gidnag takatirikit})^2$ $(\text{dhinngina})^2$

        o   Ta-kidnak takatirikit
            Dha-gidnag takatirikit $(\text{dhinngina})^2$

Lesson 6.1   Rela: Variation I

+   Dha - gi d   na g   ta ka |ti ri ki t, Dha - gi d

o   na g   ta ka   ti ri ki t |dhin n gi na, dhin n gi na

+   Ta - ki d   na ka ta ka |ti ri ki t, Dha - qi d

o   na g   ta ka   ti ri ki t |dhin n gina, dhin n gi na

    Practice sequence
                 Theka: 1 time at 1 stroke per beat
                Theme: 1 time at 2 strokes per beat
                    "   2 times at 4 strokes per beat
        Variation I: 2 times at 4 strokes per beat

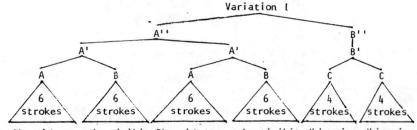

Variation I begins with a doubling of a phrase from the theme.

Variation II: + (Dha-gidnag takatirikit)^2
                  Dha-gidnag (takatirikit dhinngina)^3
                                              dhinngina

              + (Ta-kidnak takatirikit)^2
                  Dha-gidnag (takatirikit dhinngina)^3
                                              dhinngina

Lesson 6.2   Rela: Variation II

+ Dha - gi d   na g   ta ka │ti ri ki t,   Dha - gi d

o na g   ta ka ti ri ki t, │Dha - gi d   na g   ta ka

+ ti ri ki t   dhin n gi na, │ta ka ti ri ki t   dhin n

o gi na, ta ka ti ri ki t   │dhin n gi na dhin n gi na

+ Ta - ki d   na k   ta ka │ti ri ki t,   Ta - ki d

o na k   ta ka ti ri ki t, │Dha - gi d   na g   ta ka

+ ti ri ki t   dhin n gi na, │ta ka ti ri ki t   dhin n

o gi na, ta ka ti ri ki t   │dhin n gi na dhin n gi na

Practice sequence
            Theka: 1 time at 1 stroke per beat
            Theme: 1 time at 2 strokes per beat
              "   2 times at 4 strokes per beat
       Variations: 2 times each at 4 strokes per beat

Variation II

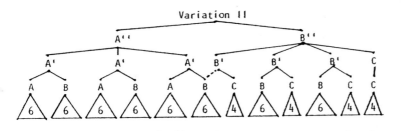

A = Dha-gidnag,   B = takatirikit,   and   C = dhinngina

This variation could be assigned many different structures. The third
B can be thought of as part of the A'' phrase (AB)(AB)(A_B), as a part
of the B'' phrase (B_C)(BC)(BC), or as part of a restatement of the theme
(AB)(AB)(A_B_C)(BC)(BC). Alla Rakha is developing this rela in a familiar way:
by increasing the number of repetitions of a phrase from one variation to the

next. This variation begins with the A' phrase from the previous variation
played 3 times.

Variation III: +   Dha-gidnag takatirikit Dha-Dha-
                       Dha-gidnag (takatirikit)[2]
                                   (takatirikit dhinngina)[3]

                  o   Ta-kidnak takatirikit Ta-Ta-
                       Dha-gidnag (takatirikit)[2]
                                   (takatirikitdhinngina)[3]

Lesson 6.3   Rela: Variation III
Medium tempo

+	Dha -	gi d	na g	ta ka	ti ri	ki t	Dha -	Dha -
o	Dha -	gi d	na g	ta ka	ti ri	ki t,	ta ka	ti ri
+	ki t,	ta ka	ti ri	ki t	dhin n	gi na,	ta ka	ti ri
o	ki t	dhin n	gi na,	ta ka	ti ri	ki t	dhin n	gi na

+	Ta -	ki d	na k	ta ka	ti ri	ki t	Ta -	Ta -
o	Dha -	gi d	na g	ta ka	ti ri	ki t,	ta ka	ti ri
+	ki t,	ta ka	ti ri	ki t	dhin n	gi na,	ta ka	ti ri
o	ki t	dhin n	gi na,	ta ka	ti ri	ki t	dhin n	gi na

Practice sequence: as the previous variations

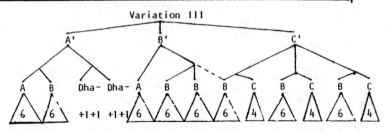

where   A = Dha-gidnag,   B = takatirikit,   and   C = dhinngina

   A tripling of a phrase occurs first in Variation II and then in Variation
III. One of the B-phrases of Variation III does double duty. It can be
thought of as part of BBB or as part of BC BC BC , or perhaps as part of
each.

   (See Interchapter E, Exercise E5, for the special fingering for BBB).

Variation IV: + Dha-gidnag (takatirikit)^3
             Dha-gidnag (takatirikit dhinngina)^3
                              dhinngina

             + Ta-kidnak (takatirikit)^3
             Dha-gidnag (takatirikit .dhinngina)^3
                              dhinngina

Lesson 6.4 Rela: Variation IV
Medium tempo

+ Dha - gi d   na g   ta ka |ti ri ki ta, ta ka ti ri

o ki ta, ta ka ti ri ki ta, |Dha - gi d na g   ta ka

+ ti ri ki t   dhin n gi na, |ta ka ti ri ki t   dhin n

o gi na, ta ka ti ri ki ta |dhin n gi na, dhin n gi na

+ Ta - ki d   na k   ta ka |ti ri ki ta, ta ka ti ri

o ki t, ta ka ti ri ki t, |Dha - gi d   na g   ta ka

+ ti ri ki t   dhin n gi na, |ta ka ti ri ki ta dhin n

o gi na, ta ka ti ri ki ta |dhin n gi na, dhin n gi na

Practice sequence: as the previous variations

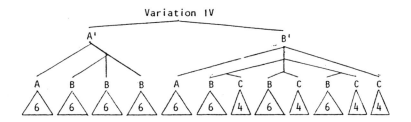

Variation IV

where A = Dha-gidnag, B = takatirikit, and C = dhinngina

In this variation, the phrase BBB has been transposed to near the
beginning of the line. It is interesting to note the parallel structures
in the two limbs (A(BB̲B̲) and (A (BC BC BC)...).

Variation V: + (Dha-gidnag takatirikit Dha-Dha-)^2
 Dha gidnag (takatirikit)^3 (dhinngina)^2

 + Ta-kidnak takatirikit Ta Ta-
 Ta-kidnak takatirikit Dha-Dha-
 Dha-gidnag (takatirikita)^3 (dhinngina)^2

Lesson 6.5 Rela: Variation V
Medium tempo

+ Dha - gi d na g ta ka |ti ri ki t Dha - Dha -

o Dha - gi d na g ta ka |ti ri ki t Dha - Dha -

+ Dha - gi d na g ta ka |ti ri ki t, ta ka ti ri

o ki t, ta ka ti ri ki t |dhin n gi na, dhin n gina

+ Ta - ki t na k ta ka |ti ri ki t Ta - Ta -

o Ta - ki t na k ta ka |ti ri ki t Dha - Dha -

+ Dha - gi d na g ta ka |ti ri ki t, ta ka ti ri

o ki ta, ta ka ti ri ki ta |dhin n gi na, dhin n gi na

Practice sequence: as the previous variations

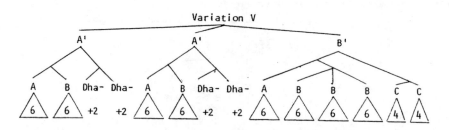

where A = Dha-gidnag, B = takatirikit, and C = dhinngina

In the two preceding variations the BBB phrase occurred near the beginning and middle of the lines. In this final variation it occurs near the end.

Tihai   +   (Dha-gidnag (takatirikit dhinngina Dha-g)^2
                        takatirikit dhinngina Dha)^3
                                                    +

Lesson 6.6 Rela: Tihai
Medium tempo

```
+   Dha -  gi d   na g   ta ka |ti ri  ki t   dhin n gi na

o   Dha -  n ta   ka ti  ri ki |t dhin n gi   na Dha - n

+   ta ka ti ri   ki t   dhin n |gi na  DhaDha - gi   d na

o   g ta   ka ti  ri ki  t dhin |n gi   na Dha - n   ta ka

+   ti ri  ki t   dhin n gi na  |Dha -  n ta   ka ti  ri ki

o   t dhin n gi   na Dha,Dha -  |gi d   na g   ta ka  ti ri

+   ki ta  dhin n gi na  Dha -  |n ta   ka ti  ri ki  t dhin

o   n gi   na Dha - n    ta ka |ti ri  ki t   dhin n gi na |Dha
                                                             +
```

Practice sequence

                    Theka: 1 cycle at 1 stroke per beat
                    Theme: 1 time at 2 strokes per beat
                           2 times at 4 strokes per beat
                Variations: 2 times each at 4 strokes per beat
                    Tihai: 1 time at 4 strokes per beat

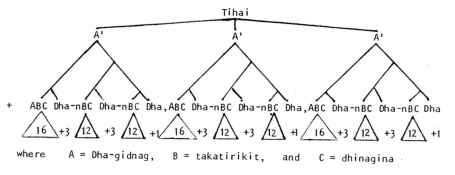

where   A = Dha-gidnag,   B = takatirikit,   and   C = dhinagina

The 3-pulse phrase Dha-n is pronounced like "don." At speeds of 4
and 8 strokes to the beat, the Dha's fall on all possible subdivisions of
the beat, making this a most challenging tihai.

Lesson 6.7 Rela

Performance sequence
                        Theka: 1 cycle
                        Theme: 1 time at 2 strokes per beat
                              "   2 times at 4 strokes per beat
              Variations: 1 time each at 4 strokes per beat
                        Tihai: 1 time

I N T E R C H A P T E R   F

New Strokes for the Fixed Compositions

Tukra

Exercise F1a   Dha kitTak ti Dha

-Ta is played sur Ta (T̆a) as in the phrase titaTatitatîta from Variation VI of the second kaida (Exercise C7).

-ti is played with two fingers on the sur or edge of the shyahi, as in the concluding phrase of the chakradar tihai of the kaidas (Exercise. B5).

-ki is played with the open hand (Exercise B1), as in tirikit.

Dha_{:m} ki ta_r T̆a ka ti_{mr} Dha_m

‖: Dha kitT̆ak ti Dha :‖

Exercise F1b   kitTak tirikittaka tirikittaka DhatiDhagena DhatiDhagena Dha

-tirikit is played in the usual manner, as in Exercise B1.

-DhatiDhagena is played as in the theme from the second kaida (Exercise C3)

kit_r Ta ka(ti_{mr} rikit_m ta_i ka)^2 (Dha_m ti_m Dha_i ge_m na)^2 Dha

‖: kitTak | tirikit taka,tiri kitTaka Dha ti | Dha ge na,Dha ti Dha ge na | Dha :‖

You have now seen the basic phrases of the tukra, to be found in Chapter Seven.

Tipalli Gat

tr kr[1] is a special way of playing tirikit.

tr is played with all three playing fingers of the right hand. First
the ring and middle fingers strike as grace notes, followed by the index finger.

 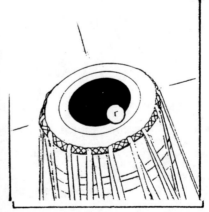

kr begins with the stroke ki on the bayan (Interchapter B) played as a
grace note, followed by the stroke t played with the ring finger.

1. tr and kr are eached pronounced as two taps of a trill, rather than as
the corresponding sounds in "truck" and "crumb" in American English.

Exercise F2a   Dha$_m$ -n   Dha$_m$ ki t$_m$ Dha tr kr dhi$_m$/iti$_m$t$_i$ ka tr kr dhi$_m$/iti$_m$t$_i$

    -This exercise is played at 3 strokes to the beat

    -dhi is played with the middle finger on the bayan and the
    index finger on the dayan.

‖: Dha - n Dha ki t Dha tr kr dhi ti t ka tr kr dhi ti t :‖

di

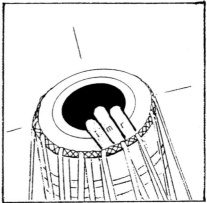

dī is played as a simultaneous stroke of the ring, middle, and index fingers

of the right hand. All overtones of the dayan are permitted to ring freely;

di sounds just like open tin (Exercise C4).

Exercise F2b   ka t ga$_m$ di$_{imr}$ ge$_m$ na Dha$_m$ - ka **ta** Dha$_m$ -

    - ga is pronounced "guh" and is played like ge.

    -di is played as a simultaneous stroke of the ring, middle, and
    index, fingers of the right hand. All the overtones of the dayan
    are permitted to ring freely; di sounds just like open tin
    (Exercise C4).

    -This exercise is played 3 strokes to the beat.

‖: ka t ga di ge na Dha -,ka ta Dha - :‖

You now know the phrases for the Tipalli gat.

Chakradar gat

Exercise F3   dhi $_{m/mr}$ ta$_i$ dhi $_{m/mr}$ ta$_i$ Dha$_i$ ge$_m$ ti$_m$ ta$_i$

   -dhi is played with the middle finger on the bayan and the middle and ring fingers on the dayan.

   ‖: dhi t dhi t Dha g ti t :‖

The remainder of the strokes in the Chakradar gat are included in the Tipalli gat.

C H A P T E R   S E V E N

The Fixed Compositions

Each of the last four chapters began with a theme, continued with a series of variations, and ended in a tihai. The kaidas, peshkar, and rela in this book are offered as examples of a master musician's improvisations on a theme, to stimulate the student's own improvisations. In this chapter, however, we leave behind the improvisational forms and turn to fixed compositions.

```
Tukrā    +    Dha--- kitTak ti--- Dha---
              Dha--- kitTak ti---
              kitTak (tirikittaka)² (Dha-ti-Dha-ge-na-)² Dha
                                                            +
```

Lesson 7.1   Tukra

+	Dha	kitTak	ti	Dha	Dha	kitTak	ti	kitTak	
o	tirikita	takatiri	kitataka	Dha ti	Dha ge	na, Dha	ti Dha	ge na	Dha

Practice sequence
Theka: 1 cycle
Tukra: 1 time at 4 strokes per beat

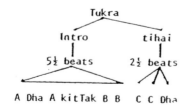

```
                    Tukra
              Intro        tihai
                |            |
             5½ beats     2½ beats

        A Dha A kitTak B B   C C Dha
```

where A = Dha---kitTak ti---, B = tirikittaka, and C= Dha-ti-Dha-ge na

A tukra has a structure much like one limb of a chakradar tihai -- an introductory phrase and a tihai. In this tukra the tihai consists of a single stroke, Dha, played three times. The strokes tiDhagena actually fall on the rests between the limbs of the tihai.

If the tukra is played twice as fast, it lasts half as long. At 8
strokes per beat, the tukra must begin on beat 9 -- khali -- in order to
land on the sam (see the next lesson).

Lesson 7.2   Tukra

+	Dha	dhi	dhin	Dha

-	Dha	dhi	dhin	Dha

o Dha---kitTak   ti Dha   Dha---kitTak   ti---kitTak

- tirikitataka,tiri kitataka Dha-ti- Dha ge na, Dha ti Dha ge na ‖ Dha

      Practice sequence
                Theka: 1 cycle
                  " : ½ cycle (first 8 beats)
              Tukra: 1 time (starting from beat 9)

Tipalli Gat   (Dha - n   Dha ki t
               Dha tr kr   dhi ti t
               ka tr kr   dhi ti t
               ka ta ge di gi na Dha - ka ta Dha - $)^3$

$\begin{cases}\text{1st time: 2 strokes/beat}\\ \text{2nd time: 3 strokes/beat}\\ \text{3rd time: 4 strokes/beat}\end{cases}$

To match the sound of the drumstroke, the bol tr should be pronounced
like two taps of a trill, and not like the tr-sound of American English
("truck"). In the drum stroke tr one hand falls an instant before the other.
Similarly, the bol kr is pronounced with two rapid successive sounds like
the drum stroke it represents.

Lesson 7.3   Tipalli Gat
Medium tempo

+	Dha -	n' Dha	ki t	Dha tr	kr dhi	ti t	ka tr	kr dhi
o	ti t	ka ta	ga di	gi na	Dha -	ka ta	Dha -,	Dha - n

+	Dha ki t Dha tr kr dhi ti t ka tr kr	dhi ti t	ka ta ga di çi na Dha - ka
o	ta Dha -,.Dha-nDha kitDhatr krdhitit	katrkrdhi titkata	gadigina Dha-kata ‖ Dha +

      Practice sequence
              Theka: 1 cycle
            Tipalli Gat: 1 time

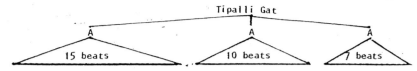

Tipalli Gat

A — 15 beats A — 10 beats A — 7 beats

where A = Dha-nDhakit Dha-trkrdhitit katrkrdhitit katagedigina Dha-kata Dha-

The challenge of the tipalli gat is to change the rate of playing or reciting without disturbing the flow of the tal.

Lesson 7.4 Chakradar Gat
Medium tempo

+	dhitadhita	Dhagitita	katrkrdhi	titakata	gedigina	Dha ti	Dha-,katr	krdhitita (1)
o	katagadi	ginaDha-	ti Dha,	katrkrdhi	titakata	gedigina	Dha ti	Dha -

(2)
+	- -;dhita	dhitaDhagi	titakatr	krdhitita	katigedi	ginaDha-	ti Dha	katrkrdhi
o	titakata	gedigina	Dha ti	Dha-,katr	krdhitita	katagedic	ginaDha-	ti Dha

(1) (2)
+	- -;	dhitadhita	Dhagitita	katrkrdhi	titakata	gadigina	Dha ti	Dha-,katr
o	krdhitita	katagedi	ginaDha-	ti Dha,	katrkrdhi	titakata	gedigina	Dha ti

+ Dha

Theka: 1 cycle
Chakradar Gat: 1 time at 4 strokes per beat
-or-
1 time at 8 strokes per beat

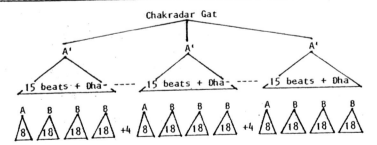

Chakradar Gat

A' — 15 beats + Dha- ---- A' — 15 beats + Dha- ---- A' — 15 beats + Dha

A 8 B 18 B 18 B 18 +4 A 8 B 18 B 18 B 18 +4 A 8 B 18 B 18 B 18

where A = dhitadhita Dhagitita and B = katrkr dhitita katagedigina Dha-ti-Dha-

The chakradar has the structure of three tukras -- a tihai of tukras. In this gat, each limb of the tihai spans slightly less than a cycle. Each sucessive limb starts a half beat later in the cycle, so that the final Dha fall on sam.

C H A P T E R   E I G H T

The Plan of the Tabla Solo

Lesson 8.1   The Complete Tabla Solo
Tempo: 2 beats per second

Performance sequence

THEKA:	1 cycle at 1 stroke/beat
PESHKAR theme:	1 time at 2 strokes/beat
variations:	1 time at 2 strokes/beat
tihai:	1 time at 2 strokes/beat
THEKA:	1 cycle
FIRST KAIDA theme:	1 time at 2 strokes/beat
"	2 times at 4 strokes/beat
variations:	1 time each at 4 strokes/beat
tihai:	1 time at 4 strokes/beat
SECOND KAIDA theme:	1 time at 2 strokes/beat
"	2 times at 4 strokes/beat
variations:	1 time each at 4 strokes/beat
tihai:	1 time at 4 strokes/beat
RELA theme:	2 times at 4 strokes/beat
"	4 times at 8 strokes/beat
variations:	1 time each at 8 strokes/beat
tihai:	1 time at 8 strokes/beat
THEKA:	1½ cycles
TUKRA:	RECITE from khali at 8 syllables/beat
	PLAY THEKA ½ cycle
	PLAY TUKRA 1 time at 8 strokes/beat
THEKA:	1 cycle
TIPALLI GAT:	RECITE 1 time beginning at 2 syllables/beat
	PLAY THEKA 1 cycle (optional)
	PLAY GAT 1 time beginning at 2 strokes/beat
THEKA:	1 cycle
CHAKRADAR GAT:	RECITE 1 time at 4 strokes/beat
	PLAY THEKA 1 cycle (optional)
	PLAY GAT 1 time at 4 strokes/beat

The soloist creates musical interest by alternating between theka and the other
rhythmic forms. The solo begins with theka, which establishes the time frame
in the listener's mind. The melodic accompanist, if any, plays a simple, repeating
melody called a lehra. Once the time frame has been firmly established in the
listener's mind, the theka becomes of secondary importance, and the attention

is drawn to the other rhythmic forms. The periodic return of the theka gives both the soloist and the audience a breather, a chance to reset their mental clocks and to clear the mind for the next bout with the music.

Theme and variation forms. The first half of the tabla solo is devoted to theme and variation pieces. Each piece consists of a theme, a sequence of variations, and a tihai. The themes and improvisations all have the same "couplet" structure of the theka -- two rhyming lines per rhythmic cycle.

The first piece is the peshkar, literally the "introduction." The peshkar theme is composed of strokes used in the theka, with some additional nonresonant strokes for ornament. The phrases are of odd lengths and so go out of phase with the tal. Traditionally the tabliya accentuates these crooked rhythms by playing with a certain elastic "swing," which should be listened for on the tape.

Following the peshkar (and a cycle of theka) comes a kaida. The kaida picks up the pace a bit, and usually features a nonresonant bol such as tirikit or tita. The main phrases of the theme can be expanded and rearranged. Most kaida themes can be broken down into an A-phrase and a B-phrase; the A-phrase provides the source material for improvisation and the B-phrase (which usually contain tin) signals the end of the line.

The first half of the tabla solo ends with the rela, the fast theme and variation form. The rela has a structure similar to the kaida, but can be played as fast as 8 strokes to the beat.

The Fixed Compositions. The second half of the tabla solo is devoted to the fixed compositions, which alternate with cycles of theka. In our solo, the tukra (literally a "little piece") comes first. A tukra is usually 1 cycle in length (or a half cycle at slow tempo), ending in a tihai.

In our solo, the tukra is followed by two gats (compositions). The first is the tipalli, which is like a tihai in which each limb is played at a successively faster speed. The grand finale is the chakradar gat, the "tihai of tukras."

A P P E N D I X

Adaptation of Tabla Bols

to Western Instruments

If you can improvise on a western musical instrument you may well already
see how tabla bols can be used in your playing. As you practice reciting
the bols or playing them on the tabla, the rhythms find their way into that
"place-where-musical-ideas-come-from," that store of musical experiences
that one draws from when improvising. For someone with a thorough knowledge
of bols, they just "come out" on a drum set or guitar by a mysterious process
which perhaps even the drummer or guitarist cannot explain, let alone the
author. One can say little about this process, except to give a few hints
and examples to get it started.

Drum sticking. Interestingly there exists in India an instrument
called the nakkara,[1] a drum pair reminiscent of the tabla, only played
with sticks. The player strikes the high-pitched righthand drum with the
right stick and the low-pitched lefthand drum with the left stick. With
this technique the nakkara player plays compositions much like tabla bols.
The lesson here for western drummers who know tabla technique is that one
can get a fair approximation of tabla rhythms simply by striking dayan bols
with the right stick and bayan bols with the left stick.

A snare drummer or trap drummer who can recite bols but does not know
tabla technique can still make a fairly easy transition to sticking since
the drum stroke names are systematically related to the hand with which
they are struck, according to the following rules.

---

1. For a comparison of Indian drums, including tabla and nakkara, see Stewart,
   R. The tabla in perspective. Ann Arbor, Michigan: University Microfilms, 1974

1. Combined strokes (using both hands) begin with dh (Dha, dhi, dhin).

2. Lefthand strokes begin with g or k -- sounds made in the back of the mouth (ge, gi, ga, ke, ki, ka).

3. Righthand strokes begin with t, t, d or n -- sounds made in the front of the mouth (Ta, ti, tin, t, d, na, n, ri).

Here is a transcription of the First Kaida theme, using these rules.

Dhage tirikit Dha- Ta- Dhage tirikit Take tirikit Dha- Dha- Dhage tirikit

ᴸR L RRLRᴸR R ᴸR L RRLR RL RRLRᴸR ᴸR ᴸR L RRLR

This sticking would probably not be sanctioned by the National Association of Rudimental Drummers, but it gets the job done. By playing this transcription with the left stick on a tom-tom and the right stick on the snare drum or cymbal cone, you get a reasonably faithful rendition of the original tabla composition, if that is your goal. Of course, the First Kaida could be scored for drum corps using rudimental sticking, and would make an interesting study of the double flamadiddle. Keep in mind that bols beginning with dh and g imply resonant bayan strokes, which are roughly equivalent to tenor drum (tom-tom) or bass drum strokes. Dha, Ta, and na have a bright metallic sound suggestive of a rimshot or stroke on a cymbol cone. Finally, a tenor or tom-tom sound should be reserved for tin, the semi-resonant stroke signaling the end of a phrase (as in "...tin n gi na").

Melody instruments. In rhythmic playing on melody instruments, pitch contours mark the boundaries of rhythmic groupings. The following example was composed by guitarist George Landress to illustrate the rhythmic groupings of the First Kaida.

I. KAIDA (C LYDIAN MODE)

Dhagetiri kit Dha-Ta-Dhage tirikit   Taketiri kit Dha-Dha-Dhagetirikit

II. VARIATION III

Dhagetiri kitDhaDha getiriki tDhaDhage tirikit Dha-Ta- Dha-Dhage tiri kit

Taketiri kit TaTa ketiriki tDhaDhage tirikit Dha-Dha- Dha-Dhage ti ri ki t

II. TEHAI

Dhagetiri kitDhaDha getiriki tDhaDhage tirikit Dha-,Dhage tirikit DhaDhageti

rikitDha Dhagetiri kitDha-,Dhagetiri kitDhaDha getiriki tDhaDhage tiri kit Dha

COMPOSED BY GEORGE C. LANDRESS

MARCH 17, 1981

PRONUNCIATION GUIDE

There are a number of differences between the speech habits of most Americans and the authentic pronunciations of tabla bols and technical terms. Use this pronunciation guide together with the tape cassette to learn the correct pronunciations. Of course, the bols will serve their function as rhythmic memory devices in any dialect.

Consonants

Dental consonants. American English sounds that are represented by the letters T, D, and N are pronounced with the tongue touching the alveolar ridge -- that is, the ridge of gum behind the upper teeth. The corresponding sounds in Hindi are pronounced more forward in the mouth, with the tongue touching the back of the teeth (e.g., Dhā, dī, Tā, ta as in taka, and nā).

Retroflex consonants. In our notation, a dot under a letter indicates that it is "retroflex," with the tip of the tongue pulled back and touching the roof of the mouth. One example is ta as in tita. A retroflex consonant gives the following vowel a hollow quality, which might sound distinctly "Indian" to the American ear.

The letter d as in gidnaga is a similar sound. It occurs in the familiar Hindi word pandit (or "pundit" in English).

The symbol r as in the word tukra is an "r-colored" d, in which the tongue is curled back so that the underside of the tip strikes the roof of the mouth. It might have been more precise to use this symbol instead of the d in the peshkar, Dha-dDhatinna. However, the spelling we have chosen follows the convention of other systems of representing bols in Roman letters, including that of Pt. Taranath Rao of the California Institut

of the Arts. Furthermore the two Devanagri letters represented by r̲ and d̲
are nearly identical visually.

Aspirated consonants. "Aspiration" is the term that describes the burst
of air which follows some consonants. In English, the consonants p̲, t̲, and k̲
are "aspirated," which is to say that they are followed by a burst of air.
The consonants b̲, d̲, and g̲ are "unaspirated." In Hindi, however, all these
sounds can occur either aspirated or unaspirated. In this book we follow the
convention of indicating aspiration with a digraph (a two-letter symbol)
ending in h̲. Some examples are Dha, dhi, and dhin. Aspiration gives the
following vowel a breathy quality, as in a stage whisper. Incidentally, the
sounds represented by the English digraph th (as in thin and then) do not
occur in Hindi. The word thekā, for instance, begins with an aspirated,
retroflex t̲-sound.

Hindi r. The symbol r is pronounced not like the American r,
but rather is pronounced as a flap of the tongue against the alveolar ridge,
as in the middle sound in butter (in many American dialects); an example
is the word rāg, the melodic form used in Indian classical music.

Vowels

Tense vowels

ī as in "beat" (tīta, tīntāl)

e as in "bait" (thekā)

ā as in "father" (Khan-Sahab, Dhā)

o as in "boat" (bol)

ū as in "food" (gurū)

Lax vowels

i as in "bit" (tīri, tipallī)

a as in "hut" (sam, gat)

u as in "good" (sur, tukrā)

Vowels

Tense vowels are those vowels that occur as English letter names (A, E, I, O, U). Hindi tense vowels are customarily represented with Roman letters as they would be written in Romance languages (such as Spanish or French), and not the way they would be written by a speaker of English. Specifically the symbol $\bar{i}$ is pronounced like the letter E, $\underline{e}$ like the letter A, and $\underline{\bar{a}}$ like the beginning of the letter I.

Hindi tense vowels are not preceded or followed by glides as English letter names are. For instance the English letter A ends with the back of the tongue rising ($\underline{y}$-glide); however there is no y-glide following the $\underline{e}$ in thek$\underline{\bar{a}}$. Similarly the name of the English letter O ends with a constriction of the lips ($\underline{w}$-glide); this should not happen following the $\underline{o}$ in b$\underline{o}$l. The name of the letter U begins with a y-glide and ends with a w-glide, yet neither occurs in the $\bar{u}$ in gur$\bar{u}$, which is pronounced like the $\underline{oo}$ in food without a w-glide.

Lax vowels. The symbols $\underline{a}$ and $\underline{u}$ are potential sources of mispronunciation for English readers. In technical works such as this, the vowels in pand$\underline{i}$t and Panj$\underline{\bar{a}}$b are pronounced as they are in their more familiar spellings, PUNDIT and PUNJAB. Similarly, if you pronounce s$\underline{a}$m like your Uncle Sam, you are in error.

Unlike the other letters in our spelling of bols and technical terms, the symbol $\underline{a}$ does not stand for a certain letter of the Devanagri alphabet. Whenever a Devanagri consonant occurs without a vowel, the sound $\underline{a}$ is assumed to follow. For this reason we have omitted $\underline{a}$ when writing bols in the later chapters.

avartan   one cycle of beats, from sam to sam

axis   our term for the imaginary line from the elbow through the
               center of the drum head

bayan   the drum normally played with the left hand (Literally, "left")

bol   1. a composition for the tabla (or other Indian drum), such
               as a gat or tukra. 2. a short sequence of syllables standing
               for a common sequence of strokes (such as tirikit or Dhagena).
               3. a single syllable standing for a particular stroke on the
               drum

chakradar   a tihai, each of whose three identical phrases ends in a tihai.
               That is, having the structure (ABBB)[3]

dayan   the drum played with the right hand (Literally, "right")

drut lay   fast tempo, about 4 beats per second. When keeping tal,
               4 movements of the hand per cycle of tintal

dugga   another name for the bayan

gajra   the braided ring encircling the head of the dayan or bayan

gat   a composition

kaida   the medium speed theme-and-variation form for tabla

khali   the secondary accent of a rhythmic cycle. Marked with a wave
               of hand or a backhand clap when keeping tal. In the theka and
               in the theme-and-variation forms, khali is marked by the omission
               of resonant bayan strokes

Khan-Sahab   a Muslim title of honor, especially for a musician. (Usually
               pronounced beginning with a gutteral kh and a single syllable
               for Sahab)

kinar   the part of the dayan or bayan head which forms the rim and
               outer playing surface of the drum

lay   tempo. The number of beats per second. (lay is pronounced
               with the neutral short vowel ("uh") followed by a y-glide)

lehra   a repeating melody, one cycle in length, used to accompany a
               tabla solo

madhya lay   medium tempo, about 2 beats per second. When keeping tal,
               8 movements of the hand per cycle of tintal

matra   a beat

1. Our main source for English spelling of technical terms is Gottlieb,
   R. S. The major traditions of North Indian tabla drumming. Munich:
   Emil Katzbichler, 1977

peshkār	the slow speed theme-and-variation form for tablā
relā	the fast speed theme-and-variation form for tablā
rhythmic cycle	1. an āvartan. 2. a tāl (definition 1).
sam	the primary accent (and usually the first accent) of the rhythmic cycle
shyāhī	the black circle on the heads of the dāyan and bāyan
sur	the exposed part of the dāyan or bāyan head which is not covered by either the kinār nor the shyāhī
tablā	1. the name of the instrument consisting of the two drums, the dāyan and the bāyan 2. the dāyan alone
tabliyā	a tablā player
tāl	1. a recurring sequence of accented and unaccented beats (such as tīntāl). 2. the rhythmic component of Indian music, including the rules and traditions of rhythmic improvisation. 3. Keeping tāl: marking the beats of the cycle with the hands and fingers
tālī	the minor accent(s) of the rhythmic cycle. Marked with a clap when keeping tāl
thekā	the repeating sequence of strokes which identifies a tāl
tihāī	a rhythmic form consisting of three identical phrases, each ending in Dhā, with the final Dhā (usually) falling on sam
tīntāl	the rhythmic cycle "Clap Clap Wave Clap." Also known as the rhythmic cycle of 16 beats, divided 4+4+4+4 (Literally, "3-clap")
tipalli gat	a tabla composition incorporating three different speeds
ṭukrā	a short composition, usually one cycle in length (Literally, "a little piece"
Ustād	a Muslim title of respect; a learned person
vibhāg	a "bar" or "measure" of music; an accented beat and all the unaccented beats which immediately follow it
vilambit lay	slow tempo -- about 1 beat per second; when keeping tal, 16 movements of the hand per cycle of tintal